HOW TO HAVE
KICK-ASS
IDEAS

HOW TO HAVE KICK-ASS IDEAS

Shake Up Your Business, Shake Up Your Life

Chris Baréz-Brown

Skyhorse Publishing

Skyhorse Publishing books may be purchased in bulk at special discounts for sales promotion, corporate gifts, fund raising, or educational purposes. Special editions can also be created to specifications. For details, contact Special Sales Department, Skyhorse Publishing, 555 Eighth Avenue, Suite 903, New York, NY 10018 or info@skyhorsepublishing.com.

www.skyhorsepublishing.com

Designed by WheelhouseCreative.co.uk

10 9 8 7 6 5 4 3 2 1

Library of Congress Cataloging-in-Publication Data

Baréz-Brown, Chris.
  How to have kick ass ideas : get curious, get adventurous, get creative / by Chris Baréz-Brown.
     p. cm.
  ISBN-13: 978-1-60239-243-4 (pbk. : alk. paper)
  ISBN-10: 1-60239-243-9 (pbk. : alk. paper)
 1. Creative thinking. 2. Self-actualization (Psychology) I. Title.

BF408.B347 2008
153.3'5--dc22
                                        2007050346

Printed in China

CONTENTS

ACKNOWLEDGMENTS

There are so many people that I would like to thank for helping me with this book. Some of you will have no idea why. All of you, however, will have helped it happen in a way that is personal to you, so thank you.

First off thanks to Matt Kingdon and Dave Allan for championing my dream; thanks to Davina Whitten for her tireless support; and to Sophie Grenville for supplying so many stories. For being guinea pigs, creating titles, giving feedback, inputting when it was sorely needed and always having faith … Kursty Groves, Kris Murrin, Meldrum Duncan, Sal Pajwani, Ed Herten, Sarah Dryden, Julie Callick, Ed Parsons, Simon Byerley, Kate Everitt, Simon Bray, Caroline Cornwell-McKeown, Jo Foster, Nina Powell, G, Matt White, Gordy Peterson, Damo, Paul Wilson, Michele Elliot, Andy Reid, Martin Cornwell-McKeown, Adey Simpson and Helen Clements … in fact all at **?What If!** for everything.

I would especially like to thank the Learning Team for always being up for the adventure – specifically the two bad boys of innovation who have travelled more miles with me than my wife, and have more of their souls in this book than they know: Jim Lusty and Matt Spencer.

Thanks to Win Wenger, Edward De Bono, Richard Bandler, Tony Robbins, Dragan Sakan, Francois Reynolds, David McCready and Tony Barton. You are all guru dudes.

Thanks to Rupe Millington for starting this whole journey off with me, and to Darren Rudkin for muddling with my mind. Thanks to Megan Mitchell, James Meyer, Cal Whaley, Jeff Semenchuck, Andy Fennel, Sticky, Sarah Love, Colin Haddley, Jamie Hancox, Tim Whaley, Dido, Jed Glanvill, Tiny, Chris Hill, Richard Cutler, Mark Fowlestone, Will Knight and all those who hail from Fownhope, especially the Best, Children and Tobey families.

Big Thanks to all at HarperCollins, to Wanda and a huge 'couldn't have done this without you' to Katy Carrington, editor extraordinaire. And to the Wheelhouse Creative designers, for bringing the book to life so fabulously.

I am sure I have missed so many but I can't drone on forever. Thanks to Mom and Dad and my brother Mark for way too many things to list. And lastly, thanks to my muse, agent, lover, friend, inspiration, coach, boss and wife, Anna. I hope you like it.

To those who dance with possibility on a daily basis and won't stand for anything but a Life Spectacular

INSPIRING OPPORTUNITIES *finish*

IMPACT

Mojo Makers

INSIGHT

IDEAS

start

INTRODUCTORY BIT

Is this it?

THAT UNCERTAIN FEELING

Years ago, I realized that the job I was in was no longer for me. I had this itch that I couldn't scratch. For months I couldn't work out what it was – all I knew was that it was unsettling and as the itch increased so did my dissatisfaction. My discontent wasn't specific, more of a feeling that something wasn't quite right. In fact it amounted almost to a feeling of emptiness.

> ## Stuck is a feeling — never a reality

I tried everything. I worked harder, I went on vacation. I chatted to friends about it, I pondered long and hard. I drank more beer, I drank less beer. I got fit, I read books. No matter what I tried, the itch just grew steadily stronger until I could no longer ignore it. It was a message telling me that it was time for a change, a time to take the next step, the next challenge. I felt it in every cell.

The only problem was that I had absolutely no idea what to do. I had no concept of what I was capable of or how to work out what my opportunities and potential choices were. It was an incredibly frustrating feeling. I felt like there was a huge wave building beneath me but I was unable to catch it, unable to use its power. I actually felt a bit scared.

After graduating I joined Bass Brewers as a shiny, fresh management trainee. I was excited and ambitious and soon found myself running a sales territory in England's Midlands. I was learning the ropes by selling beer to working men's clubs at a time when deals were closed more by personal relationships than business savvy. What an education. Soon I could sup mild and smoke Embassy's with the best of them.

I managed to escape the trunk-full of beer mats by convincing the marketing director that I understood brands and that my talents would be best spent growing the Tennents equity. Things were going great. My lucky break came when I moved onto Carling Black Label – Britain's largest FMCG (Fast Moving Consumer Goods) brand. It was the time of those bouncing towel ads and sponsoring the Premiership. Big budgets, lots of great agencies to play with and learning loads. We even won 'Brand of the Year'. My master plan was running like clockwork.

When I got promoted to the Grolsch brand, there was no stopping me. The expense account got bigger, my suits looked better and I could now control my own destiny. The fast-track future was mine. And yet something was missing. The years rolling out in front of me all looked the same, just with a bigger car.

Out of desperation I went to the Human Resources Director because I figured his department did all that succession planning, career advice and all the good people stuff; and if ever there was a people issue, I was it! I explained that I loved the business but couldn't continue doing what I was doing. He was stumped. In his mind, being on the fast-track program and running a massive, sexy brand should be a dream to anyone of my age (an ancient 27!).

So there I was. I had played by the rules and followed the system: high school, college, first job, then the first decent job I wanted. I had proved myself, learnt a discipline, got a value on the transfer market and all of a sudden I was asking: 'What is it I want to do?'. I had no idea. All I knew was that if I stayed where I was I would be in a seemingly endless rut, with an expanding waistline and ambition ebbing from my very soul.

I had to go and look for an answer and I knew that I wouldn't find it where I was; so I decided to search the world for inspiration. I threw in my job and jumped on a plane to see what was out there.

The act of traveling and not having the safety net of an income turned out to be instrumental in generating new thinking. Firstly, it created FRESHNESS. I was going to places I had never been to before. I was enjoying experiences that helped stimulate and energize me. I also created some movement in my life. I knew that I wouldn't return until I was excited enough to do so, until I knew what I really wanted to do. I had invested in this decision – the cost of a good job, travel money, relationships put on

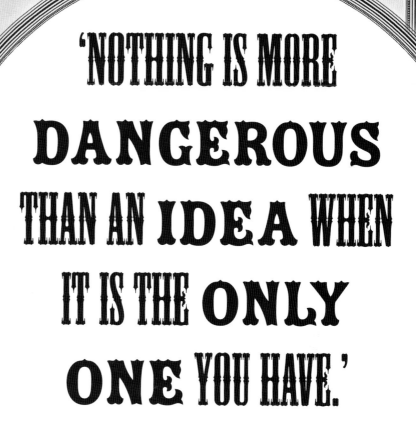

'NOTHING IS MORE **DANGEROUS** THAN AN **IDEA** WHEN IT IS THE **ONLY** **ONE** YOU HAVE.'

Emile Chartier

hold or at best being tickled from a distance. I had time, space and focus. The conditions were perfect for a big explore; a no-holds barred wrestle with my future.

Embracing freshness keeps you new and shiny

The only problem was that I had no idea how to tackle the huge question: 'What Next?' It was such a broad question that my mind just boggled. I needed a process, an approach that would help provide me with meaning.

By reading lots of personal development books, trying out creative exercises and experimenting with anybody fool enough to fall for my generous drink buying, I started to create that process. The first stage was to explore what my opportunity really was. By doing so I could then chunk it down into manageable parts that I could then get my head around, areas that I could focus on and create ideas for. I then found that certain exercises assisted me in breaking out of my usual, set way of thinking. This new approach helped me create ideas and potential solutions that were inspiring but also truly connected to who I really am and what makes me tick. Then all I had to do was to come up with a plan to make them happen, which actually turned out to be really easy – once I had found something I was excited about.

This process was incredibly exploratory. The more playful I became, the more opportunities arose. I realized that while the process was enormously valuable, it was the way I approached it that was key to making it work. As time, space and focus worked their magic, I learnt a lot about myself and some of my personal beliefs with regard to how my life 'should' be. It turned out it was these beliefs that were keeping me stuck.

Up until that moment, my career and my life's focus had essentially been fun and rewarding, but it always felt as if I was doing one thing to achieve another: getting promoted in order to build a really significant profile at work, so making me able to create some heavy duty impact and so get a really big job …

I came to understand that deep in my subconscious there was a belief that by following all these stages eventually I would achieve some sort of Nirvana, an ultimate life state, a place where I could be happy. There would come a time when I had achieved the next big goal and horns would sound, fireworks explode, and the wise and the beautiful of the world would surround me saying: 'Chris, you've done it! Stop that toiling, it's now time to party. Enjoy life, the rest of it is yours.'

I know this may all sound ridiculous, but is this belief really so foreign to you? Whether it's getting the next promotion, buying a house in the country, waiting for the kids to grow up so you can travel or just getting a bit more cash in the bank; we all mortgage our happiness. It was for that very reason that I wasn't doing something that I loved, and that was what had started the itch.

When I was traveling, tomorrow didn't exist. I wasn't working towards anything. There was only the present. If I had become attached to an output there would always have been the chance of disappointment. For example, if I was planning a trip out on a boat and all I imagined was calm seas and clear blue skies, then I would only have been happy if nature provided those precise conditions. But as we all know the beauty of being alive is that we cannot predict the future. I learnt that by all means I should make a plan, but then I must let go of it, detach and see what happens. I soon discovered that when the bus didn't show, the heavens opened and there was no room in the inn, I would often have a much more fulfilling and adventurous day than when it went like clockwork.

When traveling, I remembered what it was like to enjoy every day regardless of the weather, the reliability of the buses or the lack of dry places to rest my head. Every day became an adventure and the less attached I became to an outcome, the more fun I had. It was a wonderful game. What I realized was that back home, life hadn't felt like a game for some time. I was taking it all too seriously. And, worst of all, I was taking myself too seriously. I now knew that any opportunities that I wanted to take had to be as much for the moment as for where they might possibly take me.

A LIFE
LIVED FOR

TOMORROW IS CRAPPY TODAY

We all have a choice. We create our own reality, so if we are having a bad time, it is likely to be our fault and nobody else's. We can't control the world but we can control the way we perceive it and react to it. This belief is core to creating freedom through opportunities. When we feel that we have become victims through circumstance, and believe that people are ganging up against us, we remain stuck.

When at last I realized that every day is just perfect and that my challenge is to be able to see it as so, my whole perspective changed. Each day may be perfect in creating motivation, perfect in teaching me something or perfect in restoring energy; in any case it is still perfect. It is neither wrong or right; good or bad. It just is. With this in mind, I made the decision to be engaged, energized and optimistic about my opportunities. I was in control, I had choice. The game had begun.

I had managed to get off the merry-go-round and this helped me to see things with clarity, realize the world's immense possibility. I learnt that we all have the gift of creative imagination, but we have never been taught to use it properly.

Creativity has to be of some benefit. Some impact. All too often our imaginations are only employed in the field of dreams. By dreaming we don't advance our lives, we just live in an escapist world. What I was now doing was applied dreaming, creating a focus that meant my creative efforts were not merely whimsical but productive. I was creating my options for the next stage of my life – my future!

As I considered my options, sometimes I would become distracted by shiny, pretty things; opportunities that looked attractive but when I dug a little deeper, I would realize that their attraction was superficial. For example, the worlds of film, television and music have always seemed incredibly sexy to me, but if you look beneath the surface, those industries are no more rewarding than hundreds of others. For every person in these businesses who enjoys the ideal life of glamour, fame and pure self-expression, there are countless others on the hamster wheel of life; doing what others want them to, working harder than they'd like to, with colleagues they wouldn't ideally choose and feeling thoroughly unfulfilled. Having said that, it is possible to have a fabulous life working in any career, as long as you are in it for the right reasons, where you can be true to yourself, where it is not just another stepping stone towards happiness.

Energy IN is key to energy OUT

For myself, sitting on an island on the other side of the world, I found it difficult to know what my range of possibilities looked like, so I did some homework. I read books, met people, watched films and talked to others about my interests. In doing so, I slowly started to fill in the details. It was a bit like painting by numbers. While I might never finish the picture, by getting some colors in place, I could get a good feel for what it might look like.

Once I knew what it was that I wanted and what it was that excited me about my opportunities, the key to creating exciting ideas for my future was to fill my life with stimuli and be playful with them. I just experienced these stimuli and noticed what reactions they created in me, without analyzing or trying to understand them. Every reaction gives us some

information. Either we want more of it or less of it. If we want more of it, then create it. It's as simple as that.

Life is complex, and we must listen carefully to what our feelings tell us. If I was to spend all my life sailing, a part of me would be ecstatic, but other parts would be unfulfilled. Life is dynamic, balance is never achieved; it's about moving towards what is right for us at any given moment. Balance will never be achieved because 'it' doesn't exist.

On my travels, as time went by I noticed that my beliefs were slowly shifting. I came to know that I was in control, that there was no perfect life state that I had to strive for – 'it' was now. I learnt that big questions needed to be chunked down into smaller ones in order that I could bring a creative focus to bear on them. The more I experimented the more I realized that if I tried enough approaches, exercises, experiences, I could always come up with new and inspiring possibilities.

This whole journey began with an itch. I knew I had to change course because of that unsettled feeling. I equally knew when I had

'THE SAFEST ROAD TO

HELL IS THE GRADUAL

ONE – THE GENTLE SLOPE,

SOFT UNDERFOOT,

WITHOUT TURNINGS,

WITHOUT MILESTONES,

WITHOUT SIGNPOSTS.'

C.S. LEWIS

created an opportunity that inspired me because I felt it, I really felt it. This time it wasn't an irritating itch that was little understood. It was an ache. It felt like a yearning that had a clear direction. I now knew what I wanted to do and my entire body felt compelled to do it. Once again, this was beyond simple logic, it was visceral.

For some years I had felt annoyed by work being a discrete area of my life where I became somebody else. It was as if I put on the 'Business Chris' mask in the morning, adopted new and frankly bizarre language patterns and became the cultural stereotype that I believed would be successful in my business. I noticed the same with my friends and other colleagues. Then every now and again, I saw them become themselves. On those occasions they appeared to be more happy, creating better work and developing better relationships. They seemed whole.

After much exploration I was ready to return home and start my next journey, helping people within businesses to really be themselves in all their glory; to help them self-express, encourage their individuality and get them jumping out of bed in the morning, loving their lives. Even writing this today, I feel the ache, the excitement, that brought me to where I am today; another perfect day. During my travels, I had become more in tune with my energy and intuition, and was soon drawn to learn Reiki. Coincidences became commonplace, the quickening had begun.

I still had some refining to do so I earned my income as a freelance marketing consultant and by teaching and practicing Reiki – by now I was a Reiki Master. By teaching Reiki, I came to realize that I now had technical training and facilitation skills, yet I needed a focus and outlet for these.

Consequently, in 1998, I joined **?What If!**, a fast-growing group of mavericks who had, like me, been in big business but had felt stifled. They had set up an agency that was all about innovation and inspiring possibility, whether that was for clients, themselves or the world. This book is a culmination of years of exploration. Firstly on my own, and then more profoundly with the talented team that constitutes **?What If!** where I've been 'working' ever since. At **?What If!** we don't put on masks in the morning, we truly are ourselves and are loved for it. I still jump out of bed to work with these guys. I can be me, and the more I am, the better work I do.

How to Have Kick-Ass Ideas is not a book of science and research – that's just not my bag. It is simple and practical. It is based on work with thousands of people who have come to **?What If!** to open the door to their imagination and channel it into their lives so they can create the freedom they deserve. It is a flexible approach that can be as easily applied to creating a new and inspiring future for ourselves, to inventing ways to spend more time with our families or how to present company quarterly results in a way that will excite an audience.

I'm not an academic or a brain expert. I am a man who has been lucky enough to meet some gifted people who have taught me and I have had the good fortune to have built a life based on helping people reclaim their Freedom …

… and I'm a bit of a monkey.

So please don't take it too seriously – that kind of behavior should be saved for other books! Some of this is scientifically tested, a lot isn't.

It just works from experience.

THE BEST THINGS IN LIFE CAN'T BE EXPLAINED. CREATIVITY IS A LEAP OF FAITH. SO JUMP!

?WHAT IF!

Since time began there have been those that didn't quite fit in. Many fueled uprisings, became hermits or joined the circus. Since 1992, **?What If!** have taken such creatures off the streets and provided a home where they can be themselves, a place where they can create. These people are innovative and passionate, they are driven to make an impact in the world; creative thinkers who often felt constrained by big business and wanted to break free.

Since those humble beginnings, **?What If!** have become the world's largest and most successful independent innovation company, based in London but with offices in New York, Sydney and Manchester. Their reason for being is to inject energy and life back into businesses that need it – all in the name of creativity!

?What If! have carried out thousands of innovation projects, everything from inventing new beers, helping airlines become more efficient, helping multi-nationals become more insightful, to helping Jamie Oliver with his School Dinners project. Over the years they have inspired and energized the great and the good in hundreds of businesses around the world. **?What If!** also preach what they practice and practice what they preach. They have helped creative champions pump that innovation muscle in all parts of the globe and in doing so have become world leaders in releasing creativity in others.

I lead the part of **?What If!** that is responsible for taking all the stuff that we do best and sharing it with the world. Our clients then apply their new creative approach to their businesses and their lives. None of the people in my team are professional trainers. We have all had real-life innovation experience and are passionate about helping others get the kicks that we have all enjoyed ourselves, creating inspiring possibilities. When we started out, we were very much about teaching tools and techniques. But while our clients loved them, they kept coming back to us saying that their creativity had really improved but somehow they still couldn't have ideas like us. We then modelled the best innovators inside and outside **?What If!** and found that, although the tools and techniques are important, the magic comes from the people themselves. Great creatives are experts in getting into the right state to have ideas and in behaving in a way that encourages that state in others. Since then much of our focus has been on combining

Our Values...

(B) **Bravery** — Being True to Yourself. Have the guts to say it how you see it, to say I don't know, to get out and experience it yourself, to stick your neck out and paint a vivid picture of how life could be.

Passion — Creating the Energy & Excitement that Makes Ideas Happen. The buzz of throwing an idea around and helping it build.

Love — Genuinely Being For Someone Else. Consistently give loving feedback so that we keep behaving creatively.

Freshness — Practising the Art of Using Stimulus to Stay Fresh. Push yourself to try new things and to live with the unpredictability.

Action — Making an impact in the world. Connect with the ultimate goal, not just the bit we're paid for.

doing of creativity with the being – the tools and techniques with Creative State.

Over the years **?What If!** have worked with many different organizations. There are few famous businesses that haven't worked with us in some way. We have trained CEOs and we have trained receptionists. Creativity helps everyone get more from their lives. We are

The secret of our success is the way we are, not what we do. We love to try new things and experiment; we don't take ourselves too seriously and are happy to say 'we don't know'. But above all we love what we do, and that just keeps us shiny!

committed to helping people discover their own personal creative genius, everyone has got one. The key is knowing how to look for it.

Using the approach that we foster for all innovation work, at **?What If!** we have applied ourselves to making our company a great place to work – let's face it, when the world is your competition for talent, you have to be good. As an equivalent of our cycling proficiency test, we have won the *Financial Times'* Best Place to Work Award for the last two years, beating many larger and grown-up companies.

4FORALL PIZZA

In pizza retailing, innovation is a key factor in bringing in customers. But beyond introducing new toppings and playing with the base, what potential for innovation is there? To solve this challenge **?What If!** helped the team from Pizza Hut stop thinking about products and start thinking about insights and unmet needs.

The team got out of the office and into the restaurants and the lives of their consumers – going at a variety of times during the day, sitting and eating with real customers, not just talking to the staff and restaurant managers, but finding out what it's really like to take your family out and about.

The team identified a very simple but enormously powerful insight – when ordering pizza, the kids, Dad and Mom all want different toppings. And although it is a product that is supposed to be all about sharing, it can turn into a nightmare of negotiation and compromise – until Mom finally falls on her sword and shares what someone else has chosen.

But if you're a family restaurant with a core target of moms, you really do need to worry about Mom losing out all the time. So the idea of the 4forALL Pizza was born from this insight – 4 individual square pizzas, each with its own individual topping that come together to be purchased as a single unit. Everyone gets their favorite topping, no one has to compromise – not even Mom!

Initially launched as the Quad in the UK, this was the first example of real product innovation coming from the UK as opposed to being drawn from the US innovation pipeline. The concept then landed on American shores, was reframed and tweaked to create the 4forALL Pizza and was launched by Jessica Simpson at Superbowl 2004. Sales records were broken as the largest pizza company in the world saw sales go through the roof across the company's 7,000 stores.

WHY BOTHER
BEING CREATIVE?

The human race has developed through creativity. Creativity in its broadest sense is simply doing something new and different that creates some benefit. Without it we would all still be scavenging for food, with no tools to make clothes or to kill animals for meat. Those facilities central to our lives such as air travel, the internet and credit cards would be just distant dreams. The most significant advances in health care, education and agriculture are as a result of creativity. Creativity makes us bigger, it moves us on.

The same can be said for each of us on an individual basis. Without creativity we tend to gravitate towards the norms of society. We go to school, get jobs, have 2.4 kids, eat pre-prepared meals, buy cars, dream of retirement, start every year with a resolution that will make the next one somehow different, somehow better.

Creativity gives us choice, gives us hope that in some way we can be special, we can be ourselves, we can create our own futures. It gives us the chance to be better at our jobs, create more significant relationships, to be more efficient or effective with our time. The chance to achieve greatness in all aspects of our lives so that before we take our last breath we can say, 'Look at what I achieved, I created and not just consumed.'

And it's a whole pile of fun. Fun often gets a bad press in business. For some strange reason there is a widely held belief that being professional means being serious. Nothing could be further from the truth. By being playful you encourage self-expression and your creative sphincter opens up thus giving you access to your own creative genius. Some believe fun is frivolous and a luxury you cannot afford. I believe in business, you cannot afford not to have fun.

☞ Are you stuck, dissatisfied, bored?

☞ Sure you could be more?

☞ Doing the same stuff day in day out?

☞ Having the same conversations with the same people?

☞ Do your relationships feel stuck in a rut?

☞ Do you feel you are not quite being yourself?

☞ Do you get depressed on Sunday nights at the thought of Monday mornings?

☞ Do you wonder 'Is This It?', feel like it's Groundhog Day?

☞ Do you run away from risk?

If the answer to any of these questions is 'Yes' then clearly...

you need CREativiTY

FIRST BIT:

FREEDOM

'I'M FREE TO DO WHAT I WANT – ANY OLD TIME'

Monsieur Jagger got it right when he penned this tune, as did the Soup Dragons when they sang it so finely. We are free to do what we want, any old time. Only we make the patterns of our lives, nobody else. Every day, we are the ones who make choices. And it is those choices that determine who we are and what we do. It's those choices that create our lives.

As human beings our opportunities are virtually endless. Never before has the world offered such a wide variety of experience. We can now really live our lives how we want – not how we are told to. It is now possible to be the world's leading software engineer, yet base yourself on a small island in Polynesia. You can write your first piece of music and publish it to a potential audience of hundreds of millions, all from the comfort of your home. You can decide to live on a macrobiotic diet, learn Mandarin and never miss an episode of your favorite soap.

We are becoming global. The world is getting smaller and life will never be the same again! More than ever, freedom is all around us.

Freedom, however, is meaningless unless we realize that we have it, and then use it to get the very best out of our lives. And to use our freedom, we need to be aware that we have choices in our lives and also have the ability to choose constructively.

Freedom without choice would be like owning the most beautiful sailing boat, with teak decks and sleek lines, able to take you clean around the world – but without you being able to sail her. After a while, the boat would lose its appeal; it would stop looking so beautiful, and soon it would be forgotten. An opportunity wasted, as life carried on in its usual predictable direction.

We all have freedom, but it is up to us to create our own choices, our opportunities. If we don't, all too soon life will have passed us by. Just think of all the fun we may have missed!

Making a choice and exploiting an opportunity means writing change into your life. Life can present us with so many reasons to change. There can be an issue or a problem in your life; something that you obviously need to solve. A friend of mine spent so much time away from home on business that there were warning signs in his marriage. It was apparent something needed to change. At other times you may just feel it's time to do something new. You feel the need for change but are not sure what that change should be or how to go about it. Maybe it feels that your life is just not as good as it could be. Sometimes the choices to be made are painful, sometimes exciting; sometimes confusing and sometimes clear as day.

Regardless of the choices to be made, they represent opportunities. Now, I don't mean that in a pretentious self-help guru style, but in a pragmatic way – if you have to change something it might as well be to your benefit. So from now on in this book, all issues, problems, potential pickles and poohs, may be regarded as positive challenges and opportunities for life-enhancing change. To view them as any less is to disregard the freedom that surrounds us all.

Opportunities can come to us in two ways:

1. We can create them for ourselves and make them happen.

2. They come to us from the outside world. But in order for this to happen successfully, first we need to be clear about where we are in our lives and what we want so that when the opportunities are presented to us, we recognize them and take advantage of them.

Either route involves creativity, thinking differently and seeing the world in new ways. And that is what this book is about.

IF YOU
KICK-START
YOUR
CREATIVITY
YOU'LL OPEN
YOURSELF
UP TO
INSPIRING
POSSIBILITIES

IF YOU RECOGNIZE YOUR INSPIRING POSSIBILITIES YOU'LL UNLOCK YOUR FREEDOM TO CHOOSE AN EXTRAORDINARY LIFE

YOU ARE A CREATING MACHINE

You have some pretty amazing capabilities! As a human being you are naturally creative. And although our creative instincts tend to become suppressed, we have all the resources to change that around.

As time goes on, we are taught that there is a 'right' and a 'wrong' way of doing things. As a result, as adults our creativity often comes out more through luck than application. The ice-cream cone is a case in point. It was created by Ernest Hamwi in 1904 at the St Louis World's Fair. He was selling waffles and next door to him was an ice-cream vendor who ran out of dishes. He rolled a waffle to put the ice cream in and the rest is history. Unfortunately, these lucky instances are few and far between.

As an example of the natural creativity of children, there's a lovely story I came across recently about Johnny in a physics lesson. The teacher asks Johnny, 'If I give you this barometer, how would you find out the height of that church steeple?'

Johnny, sure as you like, says, 'That's easy! I'd find the preacher and ask him if I were to give him this fabulous barometer, would he tell me the height of the steeple!'

The teacher says, 'Wrong, Johnny. Tell me how you would really do it.'

So Johnny then responds with, 'Well, I would climb to the top of the church, drop the barometer to the ground and count how long it takes to hit the ground. Knowing the accelerating force of gravity, I could work it out from that.'

At which point the teacher took a very dim view of Johnny's future indeed. The problem was that the teacher was looking for one particular methodology to solve this question.

WE ARE BORN WITH THE INNATE ABILITY TO BE SPONTANEOUS, PLAYFUL AND CREATIVE

For him there was a right and a wrong answer. And yet Johnny had managed to create other great ways to solve it.

Throughout our lives we are trained to do the right thing, the right way. It begins with our parents, continues in school and gets reinforced at work and throughout life. We do need to learn how the world works, how to think logically and be effective in what we do, but by doing so we often lose the ability to be Johnny – to think tangentially and solve our puzzles in a creative way.

The great news is that we still have the same creative capabilities that we had when we were young – we have just forgotten how to use them.

Our brains are able to take in incredible amounts of information and automatically make unconscious connections between seemingly unconnected facts. Computers the world over are dwarfs to our giants. You can take information in so efficiently through your senses that you can even perceive the difference made by one single photon of light. This information is then processed non-stop by your incredible brain that works tirelessly.

We can then engage in a rich gamut of emotions that help us understand where our creative passions lie. We experience intuition. We even wake up in the middle of the night and have ideas come to us as if by magic. And we have the ability to take someone else's ideas and improve on them.

Each of us has more or less the same ability to create, because we are all born with the same natural ability. We might need a bit of a mental workout, but the creative muscles are still there. We have ideas every single day. We can't help it – we are human. The remarkable gift of human creativity is responsible for the very best advances made in human society.

Most importantly, you have the capability to improve your creative output every day for the rest of your life. You can choose to change your focus away from routine and habit, and instead experiment with newness and difference. If you make this your focus, this will have a life-changing impact on you.

In short, you have all the raw material to be truly brilliant in having ideas – in fact, you were built for it!

CREATING OPPORTUNITIES

As we have seen, opportunities are created in two ways:

1. By **you**
2. By **the universe** (world sounds just too small)

This book covers both.

BY THE UNIVERSE

Opportunities for us to ramp up our lives pop up every day. The world is so fast-paced and abundant that it constantly supplies us with possibilities for change and development. To tap into these opportunities, we need to collaborate with the Universe, firstly by discovering who we really are and what it is that we really want to give us a richly rewarding and fulfilling life.

At the same time, we must learn to develop a heightened state of awareness in order to notice the opportunities around us to which we would usually be blind. Often the universe is shouting 'Hey dude! Yeah you! All that stuff you wanted, that bohemian, laid back, creative lifestyle, it's here. WooooHOOO! You can have it now! Yeah you! …

… WAKE UP!'

So first, you have to be receptive to all the opportunities that the universe puts your way. You have to let go of all your preconceptions about your life and what you have been taught is right and wrong. These very important principles are all included in this book. Above all, you need to lighten up and have fun. By approaching the choices and ideas presented to you in a playful manner, you are far more likely to maximize your creative potential.

By following the book you will dramatically increase your chances of having the universe manifest great opportunities for you. I know this language sounds a bit hippy, but it's true. I believe that we manufacture our coincidences by being aware and in an open, receptive state. Follow the book, have some fun with it, and see what happens for you.

BY YOU

This book focuses mainly on giving you the skills to create inspiring opportunities that you can then make happen. To really break free of the norm and create something new and something different in your life you need a process or a system. It's a bit like driving a car – you need to learn the process to know how to drive. After a while, you no longer need to think about the process of driving. It simply becomes second nature. It's the same with learning how to be creative. First you learn the process and then, once it's second nature, you can improvise, you can mess with it any way you want. It's not fixed, it's flexible. But it does have some good logic to it, so it is important that you follow it consciously a few times before coming up with your own version of the process.

THE BASIS OF CREATIVITY IS SIMPLE ...

This is the process ...

It lets us know where we are going and what the output from each of the three stages – Insight, Ideas and Impact – should be ...

... but that ain't enough!

We'll explore each in turn and for each one I have included loads of tools and techniques to help you. These are exercises designed to stretch your thinking and your perspective so that you get a new angle into the possibilities that open up for you. The process will open the door to opportunities that you won't have thought of before, and this will not fail to excite and energize you. The exercises might not be the kind of things that you usually get up to, but that just makes it more of a laugh.

Again, these exercises are not set in stone, nor are they exhaustive. I could have included hundreds of them, but I cut them down so you wouldn't feel boggled. They are based on strong principles of creativity so try them a few times, and then if you wish you can adapt them or invent your own. If you come up with some blinders, send them to me and I'll put them in the next edition. In 30 years I expect the latest edition to be weighty enough to be used for bicep curls.

So we know where we are going and what we are doing, but that still isn't enough.

Let's go back to that beautiful sailing boat again. So we now know how to leave the harbour, go out into the sea and sail. That's the process. There are also a load of things to do under that process such as start the engine, untie her, motor out to open water, pull in the fenders, place her nose upwind and raise the mainsail. These are the exercises or 'Doing the Do'.

But a good sailor doesn't just know what to do, but how to do it. It becomes an instinctive and natural part of them. The way you approach any activity has a huge impact on how well you do it. We have all gone to parties because we felt obliged to go, but would have preferred to be somewhere else. The party could have Sinatra singing live, champagne shooting out of fountains and a never-ending stream of attractive guests to dance with, but if you are not in that mood, you will still be a miserable party goer and not good company at all. At other times when you are just in the right mood, a bag of chips and a bottle of Coke is enough to make the evening one to remember.

It's the same with this book. There are a number of principles that you need to apply to make it work best for you.

THESE ARE ALL ABOUT ADDING YOUR MOJO!

That is, putting a bit more of the magic that is you into this adventure. I believe that these principles are more important than any process or fancy exercise. They are the key to unlocking your creative future, and one of them is to lark about, so start smiling! This is going to be fun.

'To the proverb which says, "a journey of a thousand miles begins with a single step," I would add the words, "and a road map."'

Cecile M. Springer

HOW TO PLAY WITH THIS BOOK

This book is for you. But you can use it in many ways. You can use it on yourself, right now. I think you will learn more if you do. You can carry out all the exercises and scribble down the results in the book. Or if you want to keep this book all neat and shiny, get yourself a notebook just for the purpose. Every time you are asked a question in one of the exercises, write down what you think and feel. Let the journal build and be a foundation to the rest of your life. No scribbles means no fun, so let rip and fill it with stuff – any old stuff – because stuff makes you have different ideas. Stuff is stimulus and it helps break you free from difficult or stuck situations.

Creativity is about experimentation, trying things out. Some exercises may work fabulously for you and the issues or challenges you are working on, others may not. Play with the exercises, adapt them and make this book yours. There are no rules and no right and wrong. So please don't just read this book. Engage with it by playing. Sail the boat.

If you follow the book's flow and try out the exercises you will create fresh options and opportunities regardless of whether you have a particular area in your life where you want more choices, or you just fancy a good explore.

Once you have had a good play, practice the exercises some more. Practice on your life, practice with friends, help colleagues create freedom to choose new ways of living their lives.

Apply it to everyday issues, such as:

- How to run your time better
- How to spend less time traveling
- How always to keep up with what's cutting edge
- How to improve your relationship with your boss

Or bigger stuff like:

- How to retire by 45
- How to become more famous than Campbell's soup
- How to be the person you want to be

The more you do this, the easier it becomes, the more it becomes part of you. An automatic fun process that will enrich your life and guarantee that you will always have options, you will always have inspiring possibilities. Bored, stuck, average are never words to worry about again. Your life is getting shiny already!

I guarantee that if you are stuck, if you don't see dazzling results, it won't be the process, it won't be the excercise, it will be how you are engaging with it.

THE PROCESS

INSIGHT
What is your issue?

+

IDEAS
Creating lots of ideas
OF WHAT TO DO

+

IMPACT
Choosing the one that creates
ENERGY
and letting it rip!

=

SPARKLY
FUTURE

There are all sorts of creative processes in the world, but they all look pretty similar. There are some basic principles to having productive ideas that assure success rather than just hoping for the best.

At **?What If!** we have carried out thousands of innovative projects so we've tested it, played with it, broken it and started again. In its most simple form – and simple I like – there are just three stages to the process.

Insight
Firstly, becoming clear about what your opportunities may be.

Ideas
Secondly, having ideas about how to make these opportunities work for you.

Impact
Thirdly, doing something with them.

Because the process is so simple, it works on anything from inventing a new training shoe, working out how best to design school dining rooms, to helping you invent a new and sparkly future. The process can be applied to any opportunity.

All of these opportunities are begging for some creativity:
- How to get more out of your life
- How to get fitter
- How to increase your chances of finding Mr./Miss Right
- How to make more money
- How to make work more fun
- How to get more from your vacations
- How to get a project unstuck
- How to make your relationship even stronger
- How to get your team feeling like a team
- How to make sure every day is a great one!
- How to get promoted
- How to raise your profile in the business
- How to create more impact by working less

Here's some my clients have done:
- How to mobilize London behind their brand
- How to save $500 million in costs
- How to re-invent vehicle breakdown recovery
- How to improve their image within the business
- How to have more fun at work
- How to make friends green with envy when talking about their jobs
- How to do two things at the same time

THE GENIUS THAT WHISPERS

Have you ever had to make a decision that when you rationally weigh up the options there can only be one solution? You then make that decision, because, hey, you'd be a fool not to. But although it was the obvious choice, you feel terrible. Something about that decision does not sit well with you and you can feel it, big time. In fact, it feels so wrong, you sense you are going a little crazy but have no idea why.

This experience is incredibly common. It happens because our brains are trying to tell us something but are unable to in our everyday 'rational' language. Our subconscious is therefore speaking to us through our intuitive feeling, which often has a much better grasp on the information our brains gather and what to do with that information to our best advantage. If we could understand our brains better, we could then use more information, more effectively, more often, so making ourselves very clever indeed.

To understand why that happens and how to use it when creating inspiring possibilities, we need to go back to school … a nice school with cool teachers who say things like 'Don't call me Mr. Hedgeworthy, call me Clive', plenty of finger painting and lessons on the lawn.

BRAIN BASICS

Our brains are groovy things. Slight understatement there – it's off-the-scale groovy. Scientists don't exactly know how the human brain works and they still don't know what it all does. Its capacity is beyond comprehension (you'd probably need two brains to do that). Needless to say it's fast, it's sexy, it's clever. Now I can't explain all the brain's magnificence, but here's some stuff I've learnt that is handy to know.

Our brain has an enormous capacity to store information. We may have the potential to store every car number plate we have ever driven past in our lives.

> **Recent research suggests that potentially we can remember all our experiences**

So the human brain is vast and very capable. The storage and processing of information is handled by two facets of the brain, the conscious and the subconscious. However, they are not physical parts of the brain as both functions seem to take place simultaneously throughout.

Our conscious brain is the bit we have conversations with, the thinking we are aware of when we are awake. It only constitutes a small fraction of our total brain and we only use about a half of that – the rest is saved for ESP, levitation and winning *Who Wants to Be a Millionaire?* It therefore only has a relatively small storage and processing capacity compared with our subconscious.

Many people have devoted their lives to studying the human brain, and its complexity and versatility are still unfolding. As the brain has such a huge capacity and is always

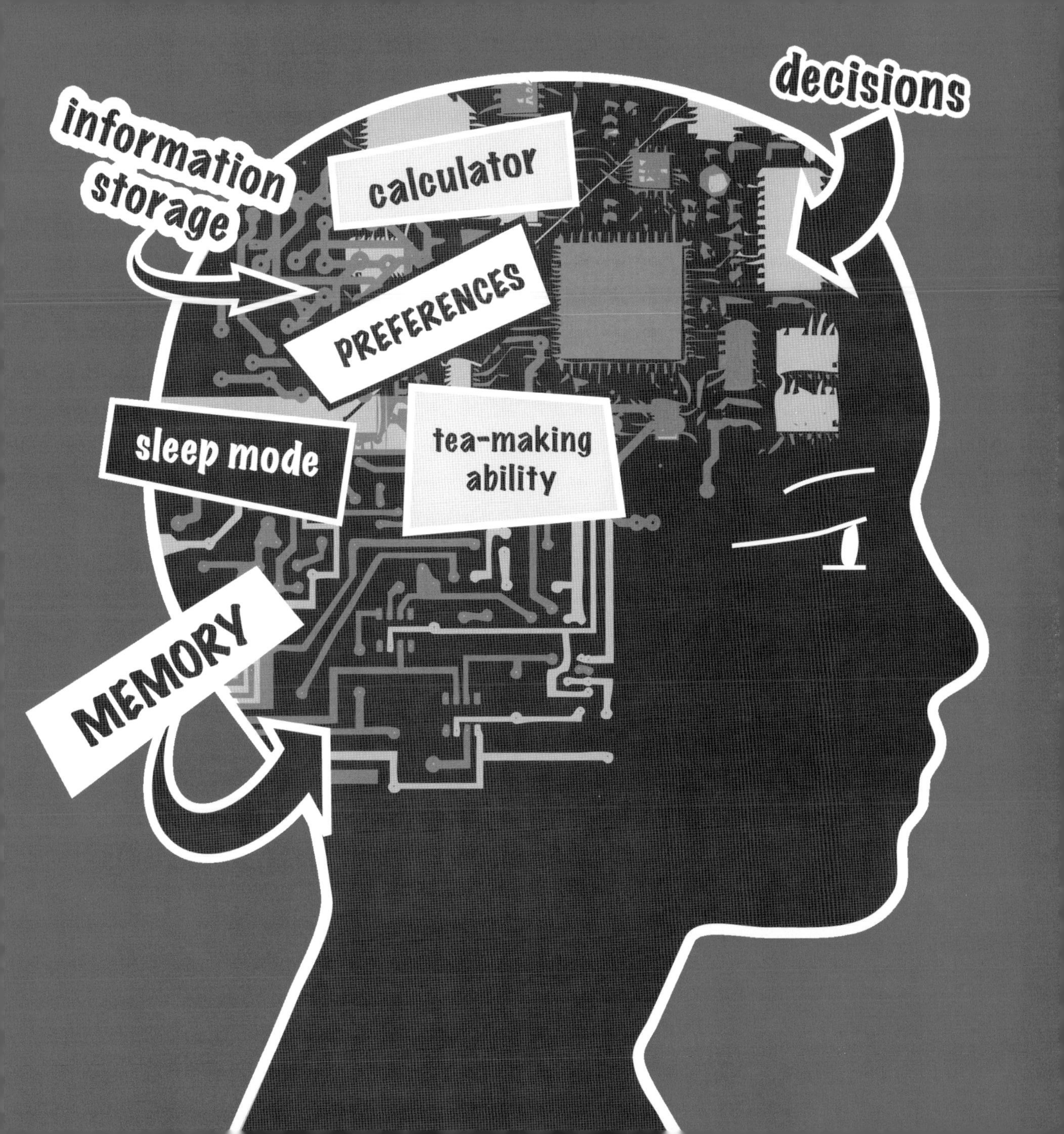

information storage

calculator

decisions

PREFERENCES

sleep mode

tea-making ability

MEMORY

processing information, always making connections, it has the ability to understand things we can't figure consciously.

There are numerous examples of people's subconscious taking in complex information in a potentially dangerous environment, processing it by making comparisons with past experiences and then sending out a warning so saving people's lives. Examples seem to defy explanation.

Our subconscious is a fabulous asset to all of us. The only problem is that the subconscious brain doesn't speak our language. It is, by definition, beneath our conscious understanding. It has to get our attention another way. And that's done through:

- Intuition

- Gut Feeling

- Getting a 'vibe'

- 'Feeling it in my bones'

- Changes in our State

'*Like Aladdin's jinn,*
your unconscious mind can emerge
as a **powerful** *and ever-present* **ally,**
if only you allow it.'

WIN WENGER, *THE EINSTEIN FACTOR*

BRAIN BASICS

Some goes into our conscious brains ... This is the food of thinking.

LOTS goes into our subconscious.

Executive pen – does so much more than just write superbly!

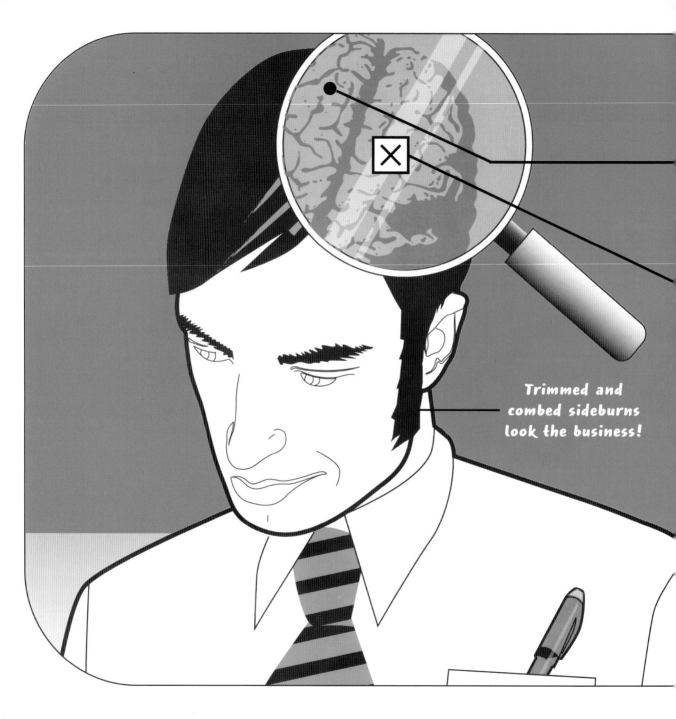

Trimmed and combed sideburns look the business!

Subconscious, lots, but seems quiet. Massive capacity.

Conscious, not very much, but very noisy. Can't handle as much.

P.S. The conscious brain isn't really a box in the middle, it's a bit more complicated than that ...

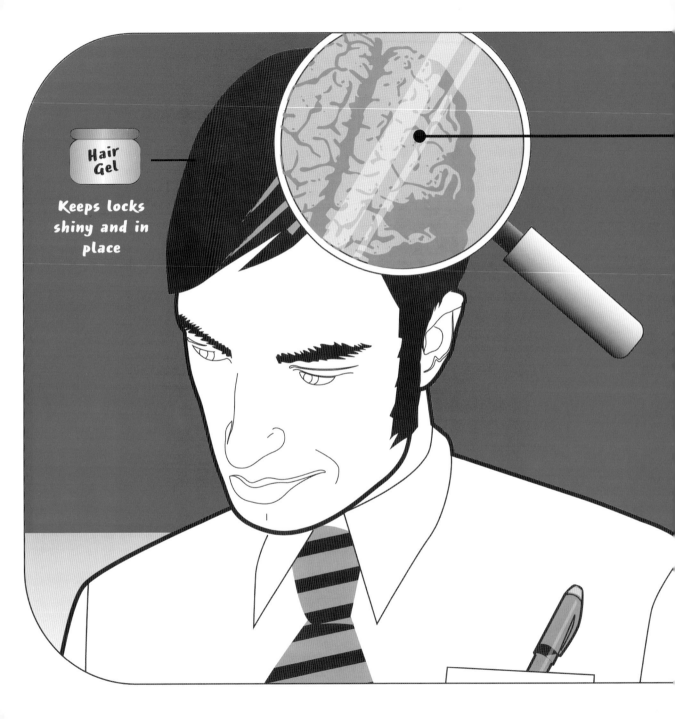

The more we relax,
the more access we get to
our massive subconscious.

Every day we regularly
access our subconscious.

Even when we are asleep, our
brain processes information.

Unfortunately, our subconscious doesn't speak our clever thinky thinky language. It communicates in another way ...

... through our state ... i.e. How we are at any given point.

CHANGES IN STATE

When people describe intuition and how it manifests they are describing Changes In State. Your state is how you are at any given moment.

Examples of state are:
- I got this gut feeling.
- The hairs on the back of my neck stood up.
- I felt shivers of excitement.
- I got clammy hands.
- My heart started racing.
- I had absolute clarity.
- I just knew through my whole body, it was the right thing to do!

So at any point, if you notice any change in your state, stop and explore …

You may notice any one of a wide variety of changes, all of which could be trying to tell you something. The fact that your mind has started to race with possibility could mean your future has just become more inspiring and new opportunities have opened up – or you've had far too much coffee!

CHECK IN WITH YOUR STATE

The trick to becoming sensitive to your state is to check in regularly. As your sensitivity increases, so will your awareness. Soon you will be able to notice relatively subtle changes.

The fastest way to raise your awareness of your state is to stop and breathe deeply. So …

- Get comfortable and take a deep breath.
- What do you notice? Write down the words that best describe what you feel.

To become more aware and fluent about your state, it is worth thinking about it in more concrete terms. There are many ways to break down state into categories, but I like these:

- Physical
- Mental
- Emotional
- Spiritual

YOUR STATE IS CONSTANTLY CHANGING

This may be because of changes around you such as external stimuli and sometimes because of internal processing – what our brain does with the information it receives. Internal processing can be conscious or unconscious, i.e. we can process information as pleasurable imagery and our state will change as we day-dream, or react to the image of someone we're attracted to or the sound of music we love. We can also choose to process the experience of a busy day in terms of creating worry and anxiety in our brains about what we have to do, how quickly we need to do it or how other people will react if we get things 'wrong'.

By tuning in, you are able to notice when your brain's internal processing has discovered something interesting. Are you experiencing a positive or negative reaction? Are you full of energy and optimism, or feeling drained and downbeat? What useful information has your internal processing unearthed about your situation? The more you look at how you are feeling and responding to any given stimulus (dealing with a problem at work, deciding where to go on vacation, thinking about a job offer), the more in tune with your state you will become – steering your decisions in the right direction so they are easier and more comfortable.

TOP TIP

To help you check in with your state regularly, change your key ring, put a stone in your pocket, rearrange your desk, stick a Post It note on your computer and use these as reminders to:

- Stop.
- Breathe.
- Check in with your state physically, mentally, emotionally and spiritually.
- Write down what you notice for each.

The more often you do it, the more sensitive and fluent you will become, increasing your awareness and how tuned in you are to your state.

cut out and keep

EMOTIONAL

How you feel. Our emotions are highly attuned to our subconscious processes. They tend to manifest in physical sensations that we then interpret or name. Think about some of your common emotional states. How do they feel in your body?

SPIRITUAL

In my workshops, people sometimes think that contemplating one's spiritual state is a bit weird or even religious. It is neither. We all have our own experiences around spiritual energy and indeed have our own definitions. For me, it helps to think about it as a sense of connection to myself, other people, the world or what I'm doing. When I feel connected, I feel in a much more positive creative state, open to possibility and opportunities, and sensitive to stimuli.

PHYSICAL

How your body feels. Energetic, comfortable and vital versus stressed, exhausted and numb. Our body often gives us clear signs that our subconscious is telling us something.

MENTAL

What's going on in your head. You may be able to think clearly and be open to new ideas or instead find your head noisy, distracted and/or stuck on seeing only one solution.

AT ANY POINT, IF YOU NOTICE ANY CHANGE IN YOUR STATE, STOP AND EXPLORE ...

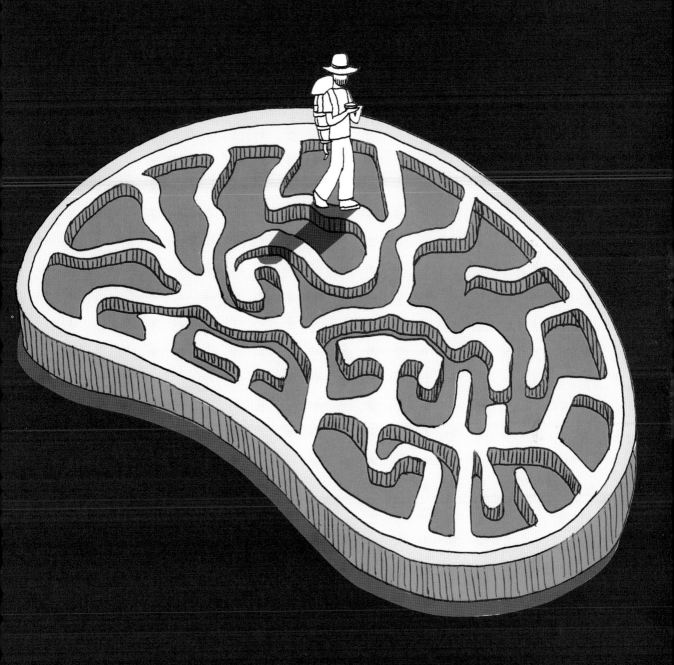

MOJO-MAKING

ADDING YOUR MOJO

Insight + Ideas + Impact is just a process. It's a mighty fine process, but nothing more nor less than that.

Powerful though the process is, it is merely a navigational tool. Energy is required for change (in fact, change is energy) and to create energy it must be enriched with a liberal sprinkling of you!! You on Fire! You with Attitude; Punchy, Playful and Up for It!

I used to surf a bit when I was younger, pretty poorly but, hell, I was having fun! I struggled and struggled, getting beaten and battered by cold British waves. I got lots of advice on how to duck waves well enough that when I got outside the breaking waves I still had some energy to paddle in. Useful stuff. But the whole business was largely demoralizing and turned my skin blue.

Then one day I got one piece of advice that unlocked the whole problem I was stuck in.

Try a bigger board!

That was it. And what a difference it made. The extra stability gave me more confidence and this dramatically improved my performance. For a start I was catching waves and standing up! Woo-Hoo!

PROCESSES DO NOT CREATE ENERGY, PEOPLE DO!

Having ideas can be a bit like that. Everyone gets stuck in a different way and sometimes the simplest change in perspective, tweak in approach or heightening of humor can be enough to save you from drowning or getting battered, shifting you instead to having one of the best days of your life.

Over the years I have collected many versions of 'Try a bigger board' that have really helped me and thousands of other people get on top of the issue that's holding them back. They are a combination of principles, beliefs, top tips and philosophies. However you classify them, I believe they make more of a difference to your personal creative output than any process, technique or tool.

They make energy! They fire you up with a positive attitude, with power, motivation, and self-belief. They make you feel alive, up for it, and widen your creative sphincter. In other words, they add your Mojo! But they do need a bit of whooompfff.

So brace yourself. It's time to power up your mojo.

USE STATE AS YOUR COMPASS

Instead of thinking it through, try feeling it through! Just in case you are still tempted to just think harder …

Remember you cannot predict the future! If you could, you'd be minted and reading *How to Get My Staff to Work Harder* instead.

You can hedge your bets, plan scenarios, assign statistical probability, but more often than not life will be more fabulous than you could ever predict. Surprise is the joy of being alive!

So don't overwork your brain!

THINK A BIT, FEEL A LOT!

LIGHTEN UP! IT'S NOT THAT IMPORTANT

There is a guaranteed way to stay where you are:

- Be serious!
- Take it seriously!
- Take yourself seriously!

The most effective way to get movement is to:

- Find life funny.
- Be amused about you and giggle about it.

Trust me, whatever your problem, whatever issue that you're grappling with and anxiously looking for solutions to, it isn't that big a deal. People get stuck because they take life and themselves too seriously. It's all about perspective. We get locked into specific perspectives because we're programmed to worry about consequences. Ask yourself:

'What's the worst that can happen?', 'How can I find this funny?', 'How can I turn this situation into an opportunity to learn something about myself and change something for the better in my life?' Just relax and approach your issue with a playful, open mind and the rest will flow, I promise.

'Whistle
while
you work'

THERE'S NO RIGHT OR WRONG

People make the rules – people like you and me! But rules are not essential. They just guard against chaos and help keep us under control. Now I'm no anarchist but you are where you are because of the rules. It's now time to break out!

There is plenty of time to examine critically your ideas when you have finished this book, but just for now inject some chaos and flip the bird to Mr. Right and Mrs. Wrong. They don't serve you, they just tighten up your creative sphincter until only standard, tested, safe ideas can come out.

And, tell me, when did standard, tested, safe ideas change the world? Never! It's now time to change your world. This is not homework, nobody is marking your efforts, so imagine whatever you want, write pages of garbage because this might just get you somewhere new and different. If you can prove it's a

success, then it's unlikely to be genuinely creative. In business today, most people are paralysed by fear. Fear of being wrong. Fear of being judged. Fear of being ultimately not good enough. Implicit in being new and different, there is some risk.

When Sony first came with the idea for their Walkman, it was rejected at research stage largely because people said that when they listened to music, they listened to it with friends. Why would anyone want to listen to music out and about on their own? Even when the first Walkman was released, it had two sockets so that you could share your listening experience with someone else.

You cannot predict the future. There can't be a right or wrong within creativity, because we won't actually know how things will work until we try them out ... **So let RIP!**

THE ONLY
RIGHT I
ACKNOWLEDGE
IS THE RIGHT TO

SELF-EXPRESS AND MAKE LIFE SPECTACULAR

OPERATION 'NICE SURPRISE'

Often we get so bogged down in the rules and the right or wrong of things that we restrict our innate creativity. Not so when it comes to the police in South Africa. There are so many rules about how you catch the bad guys the odds are stacked against the good. First off, you need to find them.

Police spokeswoman Mashay Gamieldien explained that they asked 'What if we could get them all under the same roof so that we could arrest them at the same time?'

Sounds mad maybe. But in a creative world you have to ask, how could this work?

So the police in Kimberly, in the Northern Cape, invited 190 offenders to a VIP party with the promise of spectacular prizes, celebrity appearances and top entertainment from a local DJ. The operation was called Nice Surprise. Twenty hardened criminals came out of hiding and, once the prizes were given out, were rather easily arrested. It's an unfair cop!

'There's nothing either good or bad,
but thinking makes it so.'

William Shakespeare

PLAYFULNESS CAN SAVE YOUR SOUL

Children really have a gift. They don't give a damn, they just have fun as much as they possibly can in whatever situation they are in. They are creative gods, rarely stuck, always seeing options and having fun with what they have got. There is so much we can learn from them.

Somehow, one day someone switched on the 'Life is serious!' sign and we believed them.

Well, I have news for you ... Life is not that serious!

It's a party just thrown for you!

When you have fun, you achieve a different state that engages more of your brain because you get access to your subconscious. Have you ever noticed a child when they're playing? They have incredible focus and are totally absorbed in what they're doing. When they're really engaged in play, they have no concept of time, and they forget about mealtimes. We often have the same experience when we're doing something we're passionate about. When we experience that level of engagement, we start to get access to our whole brain. Therefore, by becoming more playful, we become more creative. It's almost impossible to make judgements when you're being playful – as by definition it's spontaneous activity – so your baby ideas get nurtured and greenhoused better.

That's where creative genius comes from. So the message is, if in doubt, say 'Na na na-na na' and laugh at the world.

TOP TIP

Add a little playfulness

Think back to your favorite childhood pastimes:

Play a game

Watch something that makes you giggle like
a little kid (Eddie Izzard does it for me)

Watch a cartoon

Blow raspberries

Do fingerpainting

Ride the bumper cars

Build a fort

Paint your face like a tiger

Enjoy the power of papier mâché

Ask 'Why?' a lot

Do PE in blue knickers

Make mud pies

Spend the afternoon in a paddling pool

Dress in your mother's clothes (steady on)

Have paper airplane competitions with your best friend

Play marbles

cut
out and
keep

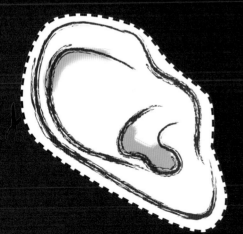

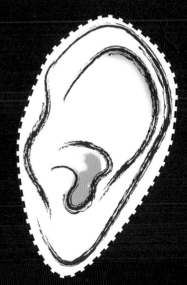

remember this!

'You grow up the day you have your first real laugh – at yourself.'

ETHEL BARRYMORE

cut out and keep

SOCCER CRAZY BANK

Thousands of soccer fans on the island of Mauritius have signed up for special bank accounts on which the interest rates vary depending on the results of the team that they support. Wins by either Liverpool or Manchester United routinely trigger street parties among their followers, so now the celebrations are also felt financially.

Obviously this is not traditional banking practice, but it costs very little and has a huge impact on loyalty. It doesn't feel like this bank was too serious when coming up with this innovative idea, but now they are reaping the rewards. Come on you Reds!

MY CAR IS A CHEESE WEDGE

When we helped the guys from 'Mad about Pizza' to be creative about their business, we got really excited about the fun part of pizzas – the cheese. The logo was cheesy and so were the pizzas.

We wanted to have some fabulous way to make the company stand out when the pizzas were delivered, something new and different but core to what 'Mad about Pizza' was about. We were feeling playful and as usual we were not taking it too seriously. Someone who was inspired by the Cheeseheads – the fans of the Green Bay Packers renowned for wearing everything from ties, hats to bikinis made from foam yellow cheese – said, 'Wouldn't it be great to have a revolving piece of cheese on top of the cars, our comedy version of a police siren?' The laughing started.

Someone then pointed out that the Smart Cars that they had chosen for their deliveries were actually shaped like a wedge of cheese. With more giggles, an idea was suggested that instead of having a revolving piece of cheese on top of the car, the whole car should be a giant wedge of cheese.

The idea was born.

When these cars started making deliveries, children ran behind them, delighting in their unusual looks.

Without playfulness, this idea would never have been created, and the world would be a poorer place.

ANTHONY 47

Debbie 28

Kacy aged 32

Kellie Age: 36

Sarah Age 55½

37
STEVE

Tom
23

Nick 31

NUTNUT 50

Audrey 28

'EVERY CHILD IS AN ARTIST.
THE PROBLEM IS
HOW TO REMAIN
AN ARTIST WHEN HE
GROWS UP.'

PABLO PICASSO

John 62

ROB 36ISH

Emily Age 25½

IN ORDER TO BECOME A MORE SUCCESSFUL FISHERMAN, JEFF DECIDED TO **BE** THE FISH ...

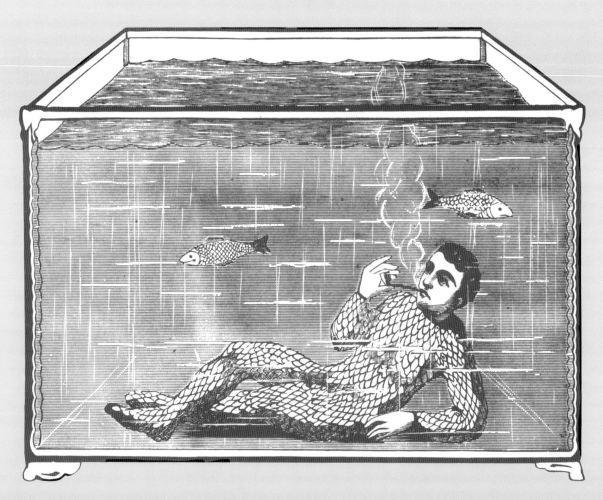

CURIOSITY KEEPS YOU SHINY

Curious people are interesting. They ask cool questions and don't take things at face value. They are rarely strongly opinionated and are therefore flexible and open-minded. They ask all the best questions. Such questions are the lifeblood of creativity because they mean you never get stuck. Instead you are always finding new angles to any given challenge or opportunity. These questions are open and full of possibility. If you ask the right questions you will crack any issue. If one question doesn't work, then you simply keep asking others until you find one that provides you with movement and illumination.

They ask questions like 'What could this be about?' not 'What is this about?' They ask 'What is interesting about this?' not 'What does this have to do with my life?' They ask 'What is the principle that I can apply to my situation?'

Write down some things that make you curious.

• When have you been curious before?

• Why have you been curious?

• How can you feel like that again?

If you are curious about yourself, the world, your predicament, and you poke around enough, interested in what's going on, you'll always get some new ideas. And what could possibly be more interesting than YOU?

TO BECOME
MORE INTUITIVE
YOU JUST HAVE
TO LISTEN MORE

1. Stop

2. Stay still

3. Take a **deep** breath

INTUITION

We all have intuition, but some people use it better than others. These include the world's most creative people, such as inventors, artists, leaders, sports people, politicians, teachers, explorers, actors, spacemen, circus acts, doctors, engineers, musicians, mime artists … all these are people who listen to their intuition. It doesn't rule them, it just gives them another perspective.

To become more intuitive you just have to listen more. When we are rushing around doing 100 things at the same time, our sensitivity decreases. We focus upon the job in hand until it's done, often ignoring our own needs and well-being. Increasing our sensory acuity helps us listen to what our intuition is telling us. In order to achieve this, all you have to do is:

• Stop
• Stay still
• Take a deep breath
• Notice what your state is telling you

If there is something you want to solve, think about it and then notice what changes you feel. As we saw in 'Check in with Your State' (see page 68) these changes may be physical, mental, emotional or spiritual. For instance, physical signs may be that you are feeling energetic and vital, or stressed and exhausted. If you were to explain what your body is telling you right now, what would it be?

The more you practice checking in with your state, the easier it becomes. To get into the groove, why not spend 5 minutes every day checking up on yourself. Once you get the hang of it, it will be a handy tool always there when you need it

(If your mind is constantly too busy still, learn to practice meditation – or just tell it to 'Shut Up!')

'We keep moving forward,
opening new doors,
and doing new things,
because we are curious
and curiosity keeps
leading us down new paths.'

Walt Disney

MAKING A BREAKTHROUGH

A breakthrough can happen at any time. Sometimes it just happens. You realize that you feel excited and energized. You know what you want to do, you feel good about it and can't wait to get started. You are on your way! Hooray!!

If your perspective does change, acknowledge the fact and get on with it. You can carry on with the process to get even more options, but if you feel way too excited, crack on with it, because school's out for the summer!

The process is only there to support you, so if you feel that you have had the breakthrough that you needed, get on with it. Implement it; take action! If you feel you need more ideas then carry on with the process, try out some other tools. There is bound to be one that will burst that creative dam.

SURPRISE BREAKTHROUGHS USUALLY HAPPEN BECAUSE

- you have changed State – in other words, how you are or
- you have changed your perspective on the issue in hand

CHANGING YOUR STATE FOR BREAKTHROUGHS TO HAPPEN

Here's some reasons why your state could have changed:

- I ignored my opportunity and gave it time
- I saw an inspirational film
- I chatted my opportunity through with a friend
- I looked at my opportunity another way
- I slept on it
- I read a disturbing article in the paper
- I went for a run
- I had a vacation

DR. GREENFINGERS

We had this idea that there was a great opportunity for inventing a range of natural remedies for children. We had been wrestling with how to make it work, what it could look like and what it was that would make moms and kids love it. We planned a big session with lots of stimulus and activities that would help us come up with loads of ideas.

Maddi, one of our inventors, brought in her daughter's book, called *Dr. Dog*. It was the first piece of stimulus that day and it made everyone laugh. It opened up the team's minds to the idea that the remedies do some of the work but throughout our lives it is the carers that really heal us, be they our moms, doctors, nurses or even *Dr. Dog*.

That breakthrough helped them create the idea for Dr. Greenfingers – the man behind the range, the reason that the remedies work, a fellow carer to help mom out. This was an unexpected breakthrough. It came early and we knew it was fertile because their states changed, they laughed and got excited about the possibilities.

MOVEMENT IS ALWAYS POSITIVE

If you are stuck, inject some energy, get some movement. This doesn't mean making a snap decision and jumping; it means doing something new that will move you towards some options. If you create movement, you will either be moving towards or away from the solution you want. Either way, if you listen to your state you will know which way you are going, and then you can carry on or change your direction as appropriate. If you feel upbeat, lively and positive, the chances are that you are heading the right way. If you feel unsure, wary or uncomfortable, you should probably have a bit of a rethink.

I once felt that I didn't have enough creative self-expression in my life, which is ironic when my job is all about helping others to maximize their creativity. I didn't know specifically how to overcome this issue, so I just tried stuff out. I bought some acrylic paints and canvas, I went to African drumming classes, I got my guitar out of the loft, I started writing stuff (pretty much any stuff).

By creating movement, I realized that I wanted to learn how to write songs and play them. I always blamed my lifestyle for my hopeless attempts at learning the guitar. With the energy I had from recognizing what I was missing I started taking my guitar with me on business trips. Although it was tricky to start with, within a couple of months, practicing was no longer a hardship. Instead I looked forward to having some down time in my hotel room. Now I get withdrawal symptoms if I don't play regularly – I love it so much! I had no idea I'd feel like this until I started to create some movement. The experience has been so positive that I'm now looking out for my next outlet for creative self-expression. Ice sculpture or Viennese waltzing? I just can't decide.

I also decided to write this book.

If you need to get some movement, try anything that breaks your standard life patterns:

- sleep the other way round
- take up a new hobby
- randomly choose a restaurant (and then ask the waiter to order for you)
- throw everything out that you haven't used or enjoyed in the last 12 months
- try vegetarianism, then some offal
- join a weird club or association (such as one where people get off on dressing up as furry mascots)
- don't wear underwear for a week
- learn to perform something – anything
- give yourself a makeover
- create a book that has pictures of all your dreams in it
- learn a magic trick
- deprive yourself of your greatest passion for a whole day then bliss out on too much the next
- have a massage – just because they are good
- work at someone else's desk
- drink only water for a day or two
- go for dinner with someone new
- talk to a stranger on the bus
- enroll in classes
- do that thing you always wanted to do

IF IN DOUBT, TRY SOMETHING NEW!

Creativity doesn't always work – it can't! It's about doing something new and different. Sometimes it will go wrong and sometimes tools and techniques just get messy and hard work. If that happens … **MOVE ON!**

If you get stuck on a technique … **DO SOMETHING ELSE**

If it gets hard, change something. Movement will help you … **BREAK FREE!**

'The more that you read,
the more things you will know.
The more that you learn,
the more places you'll go.'

Dr. Seuss

IDEAS VS THOUGHTS

Ideas change the world. Thoughts do not. The difference is that you can DO an idea.

For example:

'The sea is great for relaxation'
is a *thought* and therefore not so useful!

An *idea* could be:

'On Saturday we'll rent a car, drive to Virginia Beach and play in the surf!'
(Very useful, I can do that and would love to.)

When having ideas, make sure all your thoughts are converted into tangible, achievable ideas. The way you develop a thought into an idea is to ask questions like:

- 'So what can I do with that?'
- 'So what could that look like?'
- 'So how might that work?'

And then see what ideas come to mind. The more you develop your ideas, the easier they are to make happen and to know if they will create the change you want.

THOUGHTS		IDEAS
Water is good for you	→	'I'll buy 2 gallons on the way home.'
Winter depresses me	→	'Let's have a party in January.'
Insurance companies are such a rip off	→	'Let's form our own cooperative insurance company that covers all the people on our street at a reasonable rate.'
Wow, a shocker!	→	

THE STATE TO CREATE

Not only does your state give you information by translating messages from your subconscious, it also holds the key to your performance.

For years, athletes have tried every angle to improve their performance, from specialized training camps to nutrition and drugs. Nowadays their focus has changed. While training and nutrition remain key, they now know that if they don't create the right state in which to perform, no matter how much ability they have, they will lose.

We have all had days when we have felt we could conquer the world. No challenge is too great. Nothing can get in our way, and life is a breeze. Equally, on other days just getting to work can seem like a bridge too far. You can't seem to get any perspective that gives you hope and the mere fact that the printer has run out of toner is enough to bring on emotional trauma.

In both situations you are the same person, with the same abilities and talents. The difference is your state and the way your state has influenced your performance.

Your state is how you are at any given time and it is always

BY ENHANCING YOUR STATE, YOU ENHANCE YOUR CREATIVITY

---

changing as the world outside and inside of us changes. We tend to be unaware of our state because we spend so much time being dominated by our minds (a component of state – but only one of the four; see pages 70–71). And yet our state holds the key to our creative genius!

So we often don't know we are stuck but we feel it in our state. Our heads feel noisy and unfocused and we tend to get attached to or obsessed by a single course of action. Our bodies start to show symptoms of 'stuckness'.

We get tired, stiff, restless, we have energy peaks and troughs, and we can often feel disconnected in a number of ways:

1. Disconnected from ourselves – 'I don't feel I'm really being me.'

2. Disconnected from others – our relationships suffering as a consequence.

3. Disconnected from the world – hiding away, not feeling a part of the larger picture.

THIS IS THE STATE OF STUCKNESS

Emotionally we feel unsatisfied, unsettled, and quite likely frustrated. Although artists and poets sometimes use anger, frustration and self-loathing to drive their creativity, I tend to find that it is positive emotions, such as excitement, playfulness and joy, that generally create the best state for coming up with solutions.

YOUR STATE FEELS STUCK AND IDEAS ARE IMPOSSIBLE...

EMOTIONALLY

UNSETTLED
DISSATISFIED
IRRITABLE
FRUSTRATED
OUT OF SORTS

PHYSICALLY

STRESSED
TENSE
RESTLESS
EXHAUSTED

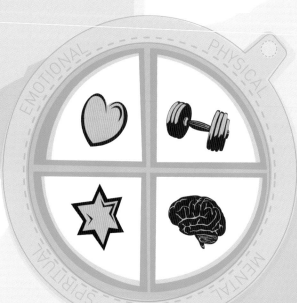

SPIRITUALLY

Disconnected from:
SELF
OTHERS
WORLD
JOB

MENTALLY

UNFOCUSED
WHITE NOISE
WORRYING
UNSURE
CAN'T CONCENTRATE
DISTRACTED

FINDING THE FLOW

Being in a Creative State is often referred to as being in Flow. When we are 'in state' we may be totally unaware of it because it feels so natural and easy. Our conscious brain becomes less dominant so we become less consciously aware – more in Flow. This is the State that is ideal for being insightful and having ideas.

We occupy many states through the course of an average day. Our state changes with every change of stimulus from outside of us and inside – what we are thinking or imagining. Most of our time we are in a Coping State. It's not a stuck, negative state but it is by no means a positive one. But if you are to have amazing ideas and come up with inspiring possibilities, you have to be in that fabulous Positive Creative State.

The trick is to become more aware of your state and then do all you can to make it positive.

FLOW Positive Creative state

COPING Doing lots, being busy

STUCK Negative Creative State

Oooh, that's where I want to be!

YOUR STATE IS READY FOR CREATIVITY...

EMOTIONALLY

EXCITED
HAPPY
CONTENTED
PLAYFUL
CURIOUS

PHYSICALLY

COMFORTABLE
FLEXIBLE
RELAXED
ENERGETIC

SPIRITUALLY

Connected to:
SELF
OTHERS
WORLD
JOB

MENTALLY

FOCUSED
CLEAR
UP FOR IT
CONFIDENT
OPEN-MINDED
ASSURED
FLEXIBLE

EMOTIONAL

PHYSICAL

SPIRITUAL

MENTAL

CHECK IN WITH YOUR STATE NOW!.

- Stand up and take a deep breath.
- Now simply notice what's going on for you.

It may help you to focus if you close your eyes and breathe deeply for each state factor – physical, mental, emotional and spiritual.

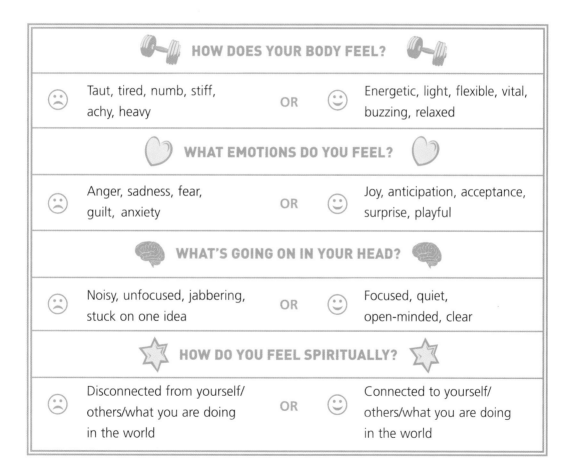

HOW DOES YOUR BODY FEEL?

☹ Taut, tired, numb, stiff, achy, heavy   OR   ☺ Energetic, light, flexible, vital, buzzing, relaxed

WHAT EMOTIONS DO YOU FEEL?

☹ Anger, sadness, fear, guilt, anxiety   OR   ☺ Joy, anticipation, acceptance, surprise, playful

WHAT'S GOING ON IN YOUR HEAD?

☹ Noisy, unfocused, jabbering, stuck on one idea   OR   ☺ Focused, quiet, open-minded, clear

HOW DO YOU FEEL SPIRITUALLY?

☹ Disconnected from yourself/others/what you are doing in the world   OR   ☺ Connected to yourself/others/what you are doing in the world

AND PRACTICE A BIT MORE

Think of something that is going swimmingly in your life. Picture it in your mind's eye.
Check in with your state.

- How has it changed?
- How do you feel mentally, emotionally, physically and spiritually?

EMOTIONAL

write on the dotted lines!

PHYSICAL

SPIRITUAL

MENTAL

Take another deep breath and think of something that is bugging you. Something that needs sorting out but you can't quite get moving. Picture it in your mind's eye. Check in with your state.

- Has it changed?
- How do you feel mentally, emotionally, physically and spiritually?

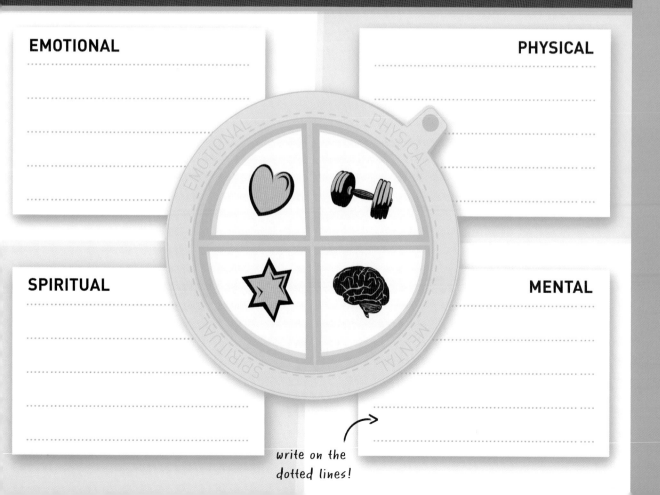

EMOTIONAL

PHYSICAL

SPIRITUAL

MENTAL

write on the dotted lines!

IF YOU DON'T CONSCIOUSLY CHOOSE YOUR STATE, ONE WILL BE SUBCONSCIOUSLY CHOSEN FOR YOU. SO WAKE UP!

STATE BREAKERS

When you notice that your state isn't quite where you would like it to be, break it!

There are countless ways to do this, some of which you will already be doing unconsciously. They don't have to be complicated – as long as you feel a positive shift in how you are, then they have worked. They tend to be either physical or mental activities but they will have an effect on all of the elements of your state.

Try some of these out when you feel the need

- Move – go for a walk, change rooms, make a cup of tea
- Listen to music – Josh Rouse's *1972* always works for me
- Physical exertion – do 15 push-ups, go for a run, dig the garden
- Howl at the moon – yes, it works
- Reasons to Be Cheerful exercise (see page 187)

- Breathe deeply, 3 times
- Meditate
- Reframe the situation, look at it from a positive perspective, a funny perspective …
- Drink some water
- Chat to a friend
- Play a game
- Go for a drive

Do whatever gets you into the right place to have ideas – a positive creative state. So Mojo Maker 10 is … **THE STATE TO CREATE.**

'No problem is solved from the same consciousness that created it.'

Albert Einstein

SPLURGE

I don't know how it happened but sometime between birth and the present day my creativity sphincter got all tightened up. I have a hunch that school had a large part to play in this but I can't prove it. This has left me with an insidious little belief that if I write something down it has to be right – or at least have some value. With such a belief, no wonder that I experience creative constipation.

Fortunately there is a way to get ideas flowing again, a way to free up that brain power and stomp on those limiting beliefs.

All you need to do is ...

Splurging is writing down any old thing that comes into your head. It's a freeflow, a stream of consciousness; unrestricted and open.

It then becomes the stimulus to take you forward, and as such, it can never be wrong.

Sometimes I fill pages with what seems like garbage. But when I read it over later, there are always a few words or phrases amongst the garbage that give me a totally different perspective; something that will help me think differently and thus help me create some new opportunities in my life.

To splurge fabulously, you need specialist equipment – a pen and paper. Now it's time to get messy. In the space provided or in your own special notebook, splurge on any of these topics:

- Areas of your life that could be even better
- Dreams that you have and what they would give you if achieved
- What makes you special
- Bizarre and mystical uses for a sausage

So go on, splurge!!!

splurge space!

----

write in here! (If you run out of space find Big Paper)

just doodle!

FOURTH BIT:

INSIGHT

WHAT IS YOUR OPPORTUNITY?

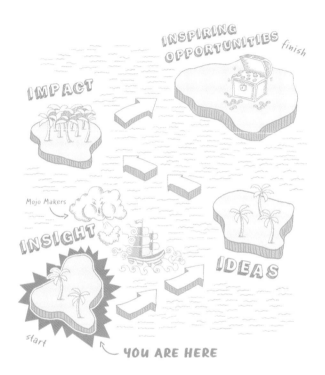

INSPIRING OPPORTUNITIES *finish*

IMPACT

Mojo Makers

INSIGHT

IDEAS

start

↖ YOU ARE HERE

Usually when a business comes to us at **?What If!** for creative help, they come with a specific challenge or opportunity they want to crack. They have spent time evaluating the issue and believe that it would really make a big difference to the business if some innovative magic could open up the opportunity. We spend time together with the clients really getting to understand what the opportunity looks like, why it could be rich and rewarding, what the future could look like, what impact it could make on people's lives. It can take weeks to thoroughly explore what the opportunity could be.

By the end of that process the world looks very different. We have insight into the reality of the opportunity that has opened up and have some understanding of how the goal might be achieved. I say 'might' because you are never really sure until you jump in. There are largely two starting points:

1. You know what your opportunity is.

2. You need to explore a whole load more to understand the nature of that opportunity.

No matter how clear the opportunity may appear initially, it is vital to invest some time really exploring it before diving into solutions. Things are not always as they seem. All too often people invent fabulous solutions to the wrong issue. For instance, I have known many people who have felt their job was wrong for them so they started thinking about getting a new one, when actually the issue was just one element of their role – maybe a responsibility that didn't fit their particular skills or a workplace relationship that made them feel uncomfortable. With proper exploration they discovered they did not need to change jobs, just find a way to make appropriate adjustments. Investment of time to explore your challenge means that you increase the chances of hitting the right nail on the head.

Throughout the creative process, there is no right or wrong. Exploring what your issue is, is just that, an exploration. It's creative and playful because there is NO ONE RIGHT WAY of looking at your opportunity, there may be thousands! Each one of them shows a different facet, a different context or angle.

By exploring thoroughly, you then get to choose which angle gives you the best opportunity to get the benefits you desire. And guess what? If it doesn't work, you can try another one!

In summary, by investing some time hunting for truffles early in the process you may find simple ways for you to crack the opportunity and make a rather delicious pasta – ok, the truffle analogy needs more work but you get the idea. Sometimes the simple act of understanding your situation can change your state so drastically that your opportunities seem endless.

By the time you have had a good explore, you will have a much clearer picture of what you could do and this in itself is liberating, helping to build a positive, energized Creative State.

BUILDING FOR THE FUTURE

Lego is the world's oldest toy company. In the last two years it has lost over $500m according to their latest annual report. A major issue they are facing is how to appeal to children who are largely captivated by video games and the Internet when your stock product is 73 years old. They may now have an idea which can turn all that around.

They tried all sorts of things but soon realized that they were going down the wrong path. The answer lay in returning to their core brilliance – Lego® blocks. The problem wasn't the product itself but the way that children were interacting with it.

Introducing the Lego® Digital Designer. It's a piece of software that you can get from the Lego site that allows you to construct your own 3-D designs and then, if you need to, order the right blocks to make it. Kids can then share the designs and even submit them to Lego as potential new product designs.

So far over 1 million children have downloaded it. With only 100 designers, Lego have developed this amazing new product capability while keeping their core product alive in children's lives. Although it's too early to judge the total impact of this idea, things are looking good. They have experienced 5% market share growth in 2005, so hopefully their turnaround has started.

CLUE:
John Dewey quote (1, 7, 4, 7, 2 , 4-6)

A PROBLEM WELL DEFINED IS HALF-SOLVED

SOME TRICKS FOR GETTING TO THE NUB OF THINGS

There are loads of ways to get more clarity about what the real nature of an opportunity might be or the kind of change you need in your life. As it is a creative process you have to find the tricks that work for you in your particular situation. Following shortly are some of my favorite techniques. They work well together, but feel free to experiment, mess around, and turn them on their head. It's all about getting movement.

1. Big Picture
2. The Flower of Focus
3. My Values
4. Blurt It Out
5. A 'N' Q
6. Why? and How?
7. True or False
8. In Your Face

The first three Insight Exercises help you develop a true vision of your life, business relationships – whatever the area you are working on. The other Insight Exercises are all about gathering creative perspectives about your opportunity, issue or challenge.

For years people have been talking about Blue Sky Thinking, the idea here is that in the Big Blue Sky there are no constraints and no limitations and this has a noble intention of helping us to free up our thinking.

The problem is that Blue Sky Thinking does not produce ideas easily. In fact, as a creative tool it's total pants! It just boggles your brain. If I was to ask you to have ideas on 'How to make the world a better place', your brain will ask 'Well, what are the problems in the world?' 'Ah, clean water supplies.' 'Oh, so what ideas can I have on clean water supplies?' Your brain has to take the big Blue Sky question and break it down into small, manageable Fluffy White

Clouds – things you can get your head around and have ideas upon.

Fluffy White Clouds are areas of focus that help you crack the bigger issue.

For example, I once had somebody come to me for some coaching. After a little exploration he decided that his problem was that he just didn't like himself that much. In fact, he had low self-esteem. Now it's pretty hard for you to have ideas on how to help people like themselves more – there's just not enough focus!

With further exploration it became obvious that there were a few areas of his life that he found dissatisfying, and because he was feeling pretty low, he started to blame himself and start to believe that, in his words, he was 'a bit of a loser'.

One of the key areas that caused this deflation was that he never seemed to do anything with his life. He described it as a series of hangovers, DVDs and takeaways. Not too inspiring methinks! This helped us create a Fluffy White Cloud:

'How to embrace life's full richness by doing lots of new and interesting things'

This made it so much easier to have ideas compared with *'How to help me like myself.'*

We came up with loads of ideas:

- Dance classes – great for meeting people!
- Adventure vacations instead of beach and beer and clubs
- Cycling instead of taking the same bus every day and changing routes constantly
- Go on a Thai cooking course
- Spend a day just doing galleries
- Ask total strangers 'what is your favorite ever book?' – then read them
- Watch a DVD from a different genre each time
- Buy some new clothes to get a new look
- Go to a hairdresser and say: 'Just make me look magnificent, whatever you want'

The list goes on and on … Since then, *Time Out* has been his weekly companion. He now travels, has a new network of friends and new interests. His only worry is about having time to fit everything in!

BIG PICTURE

To see what your Blue Sky picture looks like, let's get a bigger perspective now and connect into your life vision. You may not actually be conscious of having a life vision but there will be elements within you that have been steering your life – if only from a subconscious level. Take a deep breath and ask yourself the questions opposite.

It may help to ask these questions one at a time and then close your eyes, really engaging with what you want and who that will make you.

Scribble down your thinking in the picture areas, especially if your thoughts and ideas noticeably create an impact and shift your state. (When you run out of space – which you will – find more Big Paper.)

Even when working on a small business issue, this exercise helps give you a renewed sense of perspective and it reminds you of what is important to you. Just give Big Picture a crack and see what it does for you.

THE FLOWER OF FOCUS

On each petal of the Flower of Focus (on the top of the opposite page) write an aspect of your life that is key to your overall satisfaction. Each one can be anything that adds to how you feel about what you are doing, the quality of your life, and how much you are being truly exceptional. (It has been designed with 6 petals to give you focus.)

For example:

• Personal aspects such as love/relationships, career, fitness/health, growth/development, freshness, friends/family, freedom, cash, impact on the world, recognition, environment, fun – whatever you fancy.

• or more work-related matters such as teamwork, creativity, power, autonomy, job satisfaction and earning potential.

Once you have filled in your flower, think back five years. Give yourself a score out of 10 for how well you were then living/achieving each of the aspects in question. Now shade in that proportion from the center of the flower outwards so you get something that looks like this.

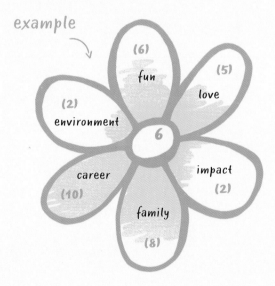

example

then →

now ↙

In the center of the flower, write a number that you feel sums up how well you were living your life five years ago. This exercise gives a little perspective. By seeing where we have come from, it helps us see where we can go. How does your flower look? A bit wilty, lop-sided or in full bloom?

Now repeat the exercise for today and how your life is now. Take some time over it. Notice what has changed for you.

If that is how far you have come in the last five years, what do you want to achieve in the next?

How would you like your life to look five years from now?

What would you have to do to reach that level of fulfilment in each of your focus areas?

What three petals would really help you to shift so the next five years are spectacular?

These areas are Fluffy White Clouds – areas of focus that if you explore and then create inspiring opportunities around them, will have a profound and magnificent impact on your life.

YOUR FLUFFY WHITE CLOUDS

write in here!

write in here!

It is time to decide which Fluffy White Clouds will make the biggest impact on your life. You need some focus so I recommend choosing between 1 and 3. If there are more, you can always come back and do this again (and again) until everything in your world looks different. But for now you have to make the call. When identifying areas of opportunity, it's best to frame them in a positive and inspiring way.

For example:
• *How to stop being so lazy*

becomes so much more positive when framed as:

• *How to wake up in the morning gagging to get stuck into my life and go to sleep feeling I have achieved more than I had imagined I could.*

Now write down your Fluffy White Clouds so they work for you.

**Remember, there's no right or wrong …
SO LET RIP!**

MY VALUES

Your values keep you on course – fulfilled and contented. If we value something, it means it is special to us in some way and it is important that it shows up in our lives. Our values can therefore help us navigate the process and choose the options best suited to who we are. It is important to stress the 'who we are' bit – they are not a reflection of who we would like to be.

Values give you a benefit, they are the end point that gives you some kind of satisfaction. For example, 'vacations' is not a value. The true value beneath 'vacations' could be adventure, freshness, relaxation, experimentation, learning or even hedonism.

So when working out what your values are, go a little deeper and explore until you land where the good feelings come from.

FREE FLOW

Have a splurge when exploring your values. Don't censor yourself but write everything down. You can then come back to the words or phrases that really resonate.

VALUES
ARE NOT A WISH LIST OR WHO WE WOULD LIKE TO BE

VALUES ARE WHO WE ARE NOW

EXPLORING YOUR VALUES

You will not feel comfortable if your values are suppressed.

Ask the questions:
- What is essential to your life?
- What is the value, the absence of which would make your life not worth living?
- What value must you honour if you are to be truly you?
- What are the most important things in your life?

(If, on examination, your answer is not a value, then ask *'And what does that give me?'*)

Examples from my friends and clients include:

- Love
- Recognition
- Independence
- Growth
- Freshness
- Creativity
- Self-expression

Once you've had a splurge and landed some values, regardless of how perfect/imperfect your articulation is, then rank them. They don't have to stay in this order for ever, but for now they can provide excellent guidance on which choices to make.

Then try this …

Top of The World

Think of a time when you were really on a high – a moment when you felt that you were in exactly the right place at exactly the right time. A time when it felt great to be you.

- What was it about that time that made it so special?
- What value were you really enjoying in that moment?

Repeat this exercise for other occasions that felt great and then look for similarities between the values you were enjoying. These will be most important to you.

Tough Times

Now think of an occasion when you were frustrated, angry or just plain pissed off! A time when you felt you were in the wrong place at the wrong time and you just couldn't wait to get out of there!

- What was it about this moment that really hacked you off?
- Why did that get you into such a bad place?
- What was the value that wasn't being lived?

Repeat this exercise for other occasions that felt terrible and again look for similarities.

Now have a fresh look at how you ranked your values earlier. Your values will now not only help you stay true to who you are as you create opportunities but also help you choose which ones will really move you forward. If you are working with someone else's opportunity or issues, or with a business, carry out the same exercise to elicit their values.

CHECKING IN WITH YOUR CREATIVE STATE

When larking about with any exercises, notice any reactions that you have, what you think but most importantly, what you feel. Use Changes in State (see page 68). Changes in physical sensation usually mean you are onto something.

Ask yourself what has caused a reaction so far.

- Was it when you asked about your future?
- Was it when you had to decide on a Flower of Focus petal?
- Was it when you had to articulate it differently?
- Was it when you looked back and saw how much had changed?
- When did you feel different and what did you notice?
- Did you feel energized or lethargic, committed or disengaged?

There is no right or wrong but in every reaction there is information, so ask why it was caused, what made you feel like that? What have you learnt about your perspective on this opportunity? Be curious – you have a lot to learn.

Remember, you are in a creative process.

BLURT IT OUT

What is it?

Talking through your issue or concern, uninterrupted for a time that is long enough to get through your story. For every opportunity that we have, we have a story. The story is our take on our situation, the one we come back to time and time again. The one that keeps us stuck in today.

Why it's good

By speaking quickly without censorship we quickly get through our story and into unknown territory. By keeping a stream of consciousness flowing, surprising insights can arise. I have frequently come up with great ideas simply by doing this exercise. And if it's not actually solved my issue, I have always got a much better insight into what my opportunity actually is. And by talking to a friend, you have a witness to your blurt. This changes your relationship with what you say and increases your level of engagement and sensitivity to the opportunity.

DOING IT ✓

1. Find a friend who is a good listener.

2. Talk to them about the opportunity you have. You must talk uninterrupted, fast and uncensored for 7 minutes 26 seconds (approx.). This can seem like a long time, but it is key to keeping going.

3. Your friend jots down 3 or 4 things they have heard that seem key, interesting, weird or just plain funny. They are not taking dictation, they focus on you and what you are saying, and that means eye contact!

4. Your friend then talks to you for 3 minutes about all they heard. They may well play back their ideas about it too. That's cool. Usually their observations take a minute or so, and this can be a great stimulus. Encourage them to blurt as you did.

5. You then speak for 2 minutes about where you're at – in other words, what you now think.

6. Write down what you have learnt about the issue and any ideas you have had.

7. Have a cup of tea and ponder … Mmm, nice.

**I have tried this exercise by talking to myself, but it is by no means as effective …
and people look at you funny on the bus.**

'SOME PEOPLE STORM IMAGINARY
ALPS ALL OF THEIR LIVES AND DIE IN THE
FOOTHILLS CURSING DIFFICULTIES
THAT DO NOT EXIST.'

ANON

A 'N' Q

What is it?

A technique for flushing out what is in our head that we may not have articulated before. We do this by creating ideas we can react to.

Why it's good

We often don't know exactly what opportunity is being presented to us! We might have some insight into it but not enough to nail it. By making the issue real and bringing it to life by having tangible ideas (not thoughts, but stuff we can do; see page 105), we then have something to react against. This is also a blinding technique when cracking someone else's issue. And not only that – by doing it with others you will learn how to do it for yourself.

When we work with clients, they often have many contexts in their head that haven't been articulated. This tool helps to draw them out. And on a more personal level, next time you have somebody who comes to you for help, try this exercise out. Imagine always being able to help out friends, colleagues and whiny dinner-party guests. Never again will you feel frustrated when people come to you with problems because you will have a way to help them move forward. Nothing feels better than helping someone move towards inspiring possibilities – well, apart from a hot bath after four days in a cold, soggy tent.

DOING IT

1. Come up with loads of ideas (not thoughts) on how to make the most of this opportunity and write them on Post-It notes or little scraps of paper.
2. Take a piece of paper and draw a circle on it.
3. Then take each idea in turn, write it down and ask yourself, 'How well does this help me make the most of this opportunity?'
4. Then place it on the piece of paper in relation to the circle. The center of the circle is bang on, do-able, safe, fertile. Outside the circle is off-brief, doesn't work. Between the center and the circle's edge has potential but needs exploration. Put the piece of paper where you think it should lie.
5. Then ask the key question 'WHY?' have you placed it there.
6. Note down the answer. This will give you key information:
   - Constraints
   - Rules
   - Visions of Success

Sometimes this process is even enough to come up with fabulous ideas that will really move you forward.

If you find that all your ideas are within the circle, it's time to go a little crazy. If you don't dismiss some ideas by having them outside the circle, you will never know where your boundaries are so get playful and push the edges!

So What Do We Know Now?

Every time we asked *'Why?'* we got some new information about the opportunity. We learnt some success factors, such as we need to feel good. We have also learnt about some constraints, such as the realities of the situation that we can't or don't want to change right now.

SUCCESS FACTORS	CONSTRAINTS
Variety	$ for vacations not buying property
Flexibility	6 weeks total per year
Short vs long vs weekends	
Control over decisions	Limited control over decisions
Spontaneity	Safety

working example ...

HOW DO I MAKE SURE I TAKE ALL MY VACATION?

Pay travel consultant to sort out 6 weeks vacation over 12 months
? • I like to make decisions
• Enjoy discussion
• Sounds expensive

Book in 4 weeks now, 2 weeks and 2X1 week. Book in 3 long weekends. 1 Floating week
? • Forward planning
• Flexibility
• Short vs long vs weekends
Feels Good!!

Book in my diary now for next 12 months
? • Would work but lacks spontaneity
• Hate feeling trapped

Buy a vacation home
? • Like variety
• No money

Book 2 weeks off every 4 months then take last minute deal
? • Would work but too risky - might be awful

145

WHY? AND HOW?

What is it?

A way of thoroughly exploring what the reality of your opportunity or issue might be through playful questioning.

Why it's good

By simply asking *'Why?'* we have to question what our opportunity is all about. In effect, it makes the opportunity broader.

For example, my opportunity may be:
  'How could I get more money?'

If I ask *'Why?'* It might go a bit like this:
  So I can get a car.

  Why do you need the car?
  So I can go where I want when I want.

  Why is that important?
  So I can be independent.

  Why is that important?
  So I can experience more, and live life a bit.

  Why is that important?
  So I can learn more about who I am and what is important to me.

You can keep asking *'Why?'* until the answers start getting a bit big – for instance, 'So I can self-actualize!'

By asking *'How?'* we start to invent potential solutions to it. So:

  'How could I get more money?'

Potential solutions might include: get promoted, teach tennis at weekends, invest in stock options, ask my parents for a loan, go to a casino, sell some things I don't need anymore, cut down on my spending. Some of these ideas will be great, some terrible. It doesn't matter – they all act as a stimulus to look at your issue differently.

So now ask:

'How could I get a car?'

Your answers might be: work nights as a taxi driver, borrow my friend's car, buy one with my sister, hire one, buy a really old one and learn how to do it up, win one, work for Hertz car rental, etc.

Then:

'How could I go wherever I want whenever I want?'

Possible answers to this might be: take the bus, hitch-hike, cycle, become fit and run everywhere, rollerblade, buy a moped, get a part-time job and then have more time to get where I want to.

Keep asking *'How?'* for each answer to the *'Why'* questions. For instance:

'How to become independent?'
'How to experience more and live life a bit?'

DOING IT ✓

Start by writing down your opportunity as a question in the center of a big piece of paper.

For example:
• I can't find great people
• I don't have enough clients

become:
• *'How can I recruit top talent?'*
• *'How to get more clients?'*

Then you ask the BIG QUESTION … *Why?*

By asking *'Why?'* and *'How?'* enough times you could cover the planet with paper and scrawl. This is not good as it's messy and not tree loving. So stop asking questions when you feel you have uncovered enough of the opportunity or situation to know what it is really about. You will know this when your state changes, when you have a feeling that you are getting to the nub of the issue. This is not science, it's instinct, so go with your gut. Then write down what you now feel about things.

Continue to be playful and have fun! It's important to get some ridiculous ideas out there to help provoke your thinking. *'Sack everyone we've got'* is unlikely to be the answer but it does make one ask *'How can I change the fundamentals of the current business instantly?'* At the least this could open up some novel avenues.

You can apply this process to any kind of problem. Another example might be:

'How to save time commuting so that I spend more time doing the things I want to do.'

You can play around with solutions to establish where your reality boundaries are. For example, hiring a helicopter or learning to teleport are somewhat unrealistic but you can move across the spectrum of realistic and ridiculous:

- Move the office to my home (i.e. work from home)
- Take my family to work with me
- Invent a mobile office so that I could work while I travel
- Move closer to the office
- Share taxis with colleagues so that I could afford the luxury of car travel into work and start my meetings as soon as I get in the taxi
- Change jobs and move to the country where commuting to work is fast and hassle-free
- Have a sleeping bag in the office so that during the week I could extend my working time

The important thing is to get your ideas flowing.

There's enough time to be serious – and it isn't right now!

To make it fun again, something we are proud of.

5 Why? So we can do great work and not worry about the money.

4 Why? So our business gets better.

3 Why? So the standard of our people gets better.

2

1

How can I recruit great talent?

start here

How?

6 Spend 50% of my time recruiting.

How?

How? How? How?

7
Develop our people better.
Improve our management systems.
Sack everyone we've got.

9

Overhaul our product range.
Reposition our offering.
Invest in new equipment.
New offices.

8

We review how we are living
our values every week.
We have freelance staff and
cut down on overheads.

Everyone has to spend 20% of their
time on a pet project that is
unrelated to their role. We only work
on projects we think will have a
positive impact in the world.

10

For every
statement, idea or
question, you can ask
WHY?(2-5) & HOW?
(6-10) again and again
and again ...

TRUE OR FALSE

What is it?

A process that helps you find out what is true and what is false about you and your issue or concern. Many schools of personal development use techniques based on the these principles to uncover what tricks your mind may be playing on you. I love this technique because of its power in helping us to determine where to spend our creative energies.

Why it's good

In today's society we often find that our minds work at 100 mph – they are like toddlers who have OD'd on sugary drinks and just can't keep still. Within all this chaos our minds are telling us things; this is our internal dialogue or 'voices in our heads'. Listen now to what the voices are saying.

These voices do this to try and help us and are actually on our side, trying to give us information that we might need. The problem is, they distort the truth so the 'voices in our heads' are often anything but true. Our minds are exceptional at making up fibs and telling ourselves little lies!

This is going on constantly which is a real drag when you are attempting to get to grips with potential opportunities. Sometimes it is so difficult to know what is true and what is not that it becomes impossible to find out what the real opportunity is and why it is currently not happening.

DOING IT ✓

It's time to listen to the 'voices'. To flush these out we need the help of your angels and devils, the ones who sit on either shoulder and whisper sweet nothings.

Devil

First, get all pissed off, negative and devilish (have fun with this – I'm sure the devil would). Next, with no censoring, write down everything about your issue or challenge from a weasely negative point of view. It's fun to be wicked when deep down you're a moonbeam! Don't analyze or restrict yourself, just scribble wildly. Check out the example on the next page to see how you can phrase things.

Angel

Now, to balance things up a bit, do it from your Angel's perspective. Be loving and nurturing, see the good and be optimistic. It might feel odd, but just go for it anyway. Again, splurge away!

By now, you should have two lots of outpourings. I fill pages when I do this – the more the better.

Crunch Time

Firstly, get into a positive state. Shake off your Angels and Devils. Stand up, picture yourself feeling confident and strong, and feel it in your body. Read through each statement and ask. 'Is that True, False or Don't Know?'

True is something that is provable. It should stand up in a court of law. There is no judgement involved, it is TRUTH. False is the stuff you know deep down is GARBAGE. Watch out here because your brain is tricky and will often phrase things in a nebulous and airy-fairy way that sounds true. Be strict – if it is not absolutely True it can only be False or Don't Know.

Sometimes you will find statements that could be True but you are not absolutely certain. If it is prediction – for instance, 'I will be less successful' – it can at best be a Don't Know because you cannot tell the future. However, 'Everyone will hate me' is False because there is no way it can be true. If in doubt, write the statement again using language that is definitely True.

Watch out for the Devil coming back. Be strong and centered, and now write what is True. Once you have carried out this exercise, you may notice a change in your state. By seeing what is True and False your issue will have changed, sometimes dramatically. With this new perception, write down your issue NOW! Here are a couple of examples from me.

Getting Fit

Devil		Angel	
'I can't be bothered to stick at it.'	FALSE	'It's good for you.'	TRUE
'It won't last long anyway.'	DON'T KNOW	'When I'm fit, I feel better	
'It's hard work.'	DON'T KNOW	about myself.'	TRUE
'It's no fun.'	FALSE	'I love some sports.'	TRUE
'I'll only be disappointed.'	DON'T KNOW	'I can do a little every day.'	TRUE
'It's a waste of time.'	FALSE	'Exercising gives me more energy.'	TRUE
'I won't notice the difference.'	FALSE	'I want to be fitter.'	TRUE
'It takes lots of time.'	FALSE	'I'll look great in my tight shirts.'	DON'T KNOW
'I don't want it to be a fad.'	TRUE	'I feel good in my tight	
'It takes effort.'	TRUE	shirts when I'm buff.'	TRUE

I am constantly surprised by how much garbage is in my head.

All the False statements can now be re-written in a way that is True

as I have demonstrated on the 'Devil' side.

Worrying about Giving a Presentation

Devil		Angel	
'I haven't prepared enough.'	FALSE	'I know this stuff better than anyone.'	TRUE
'I'm out of my depth.'	FALSE	'This is a great opportunity for me to	
'I'll really mess this up.'	FALSE	show what I can do.'	TRUE
'They will catch me out and make me		'They want me to do well.'	TRUE
look stupid.'	FALSE	'I'll have all their attention, feel the power.'	TRUE
'I'll go blank and forget everything		'If I set it up my way, the whole	
I've prepared.'	DON'T KNOW	session will be fun.'	TRUE
'They want it to go wrong.'	FALSE	'I can do it my way.'	TRUE
'They'd love for me to look stupid.'	FALSE	'I can give them a great experience	
'I'll never live this down.'	FALSE	compared to the rest of their days.'	TRUE
'My career here is over.'	FALSE	'I can learn from this, and get	
'I'm not good enough.'	FALSE	better each time.'	TRUE
		'I can wear my new suit, sexy!'	TRUE
		'It gives me a chance to hang out	
		with the boss.'	TRUE
		'I can use this chance to get their	
		input and make it better.'	TRUE

In this case, the only Don't Know was 'I'll go blank …', so all I need to do is make sure I've got some prompt cards and stay relaxed. Now I am able to feel very different about my opportunity and I have some new ideas on how to get the most out of it.

KISSING THE FISH

For as long as I can remember, I hated fish. Not as a species but as a tasty morsel. Every time I was offered some at a dinner I turned up my nose and felt a tad queasy. To me fish stank. It was smelly, vile-tasting mush. It had bones in it that were obviously there to kill you, and anything that smelt fishy clearly couldn't have been designed for human consumption.

The only problem was, I kept going to restaurants – especially when I was on vacation – where I saw people eating fish and looking as if they were close to orgasm. Their faces contorted with ecstasy and, quite frankly, I felt like I was missing out. Could I be that wrong?

So, partial to feeling good myself, I found myself on vacation with some great friends. When they described their favorite things as 'brown sandy feet and fresh seafood' I knew it was time to see whether my revulsion of fish was founded in reality or whether for all these years I had been depriving myself of one of life's rich treats.

We asked the waiter to bring a selection of his freshest and finest fish. I was nervous, palms sweating and kind of anxious about throwing up in the middle of the restaurant.

'Mark Twain used to say that it was possible to learn too much from experience. A cat, he said, that had squatted once on a hot stove lid would never sit down on a hot stove lid again. The trouble was that it would never sit down on a cold one either.'

Isaac Asimov

After steadying myself with some rosé wine, the fish arrived on a huge platter, and I swear the biggest one was winking at me.

It was delicious! Since then I have been a fish lover and now my favorite things are 'brown sandy feet and fresh seafood'.

Many years ago I must have had a bad experience with fish. As often happens, I had then exaggerated this experience to the extent that I even felt ill when I smelt it and had come to believe that all fish were the same.

People often do this. We take a piece of information or an experience and mess with it until what we believe in our heads is just not true. We don't do this consciously, it just seems to happen until the belief is so strong we have no choice but to react to it.

You may find that when you are thinking about your situation, you hold a few beliefs about it that aren't quite true. If you can spot these delusions, you will have way more freedom.
Just like me. And fish are now my friends.
(You can keep them whelks, though!)

IN YOUR FACE

What is it?

A way of keeping the issue at the front of your mind. Physically represent your issue and any options that you may have, around your everyday environment, in your bathroom, in your car, in your wallet, by your TV.

Why it's good

Our brains often become attuned to focus upon certain things – this is called 'selective attention'. For instance, you may find that when you order a new car, everywhere you go you see the same make, model and even color that you ordered. In a similar way, when women are pregnant they often notice more children and other pregnant women. Are there actually more? No. Their brain has been programmed to be more conscious of them and therefore sees them more readily. By making your opportunity In Your Face, you will achieve much the same thing.

Your brain will then make connections more readily with the world around you and help you come up with more and better ideas for more of the time. Your subconscious brain will use your physical reminders in its constant processing, so giving you a much higher chance of a breakthrough.

People often spend time at the weekend or on vacation thinking about their life and opportunities. Then they go to work and get busy and the next thing they know weeks, months, even years have gone by and no time has been spent coming up with solutions. They are needlessly stuck. By making your issue In Your Face, you take the bull by the horns and create a bit of magic.

The first time I used this trick I thought magic was happening. When traveling in New Zealand, I was fortunate enough to swim with wild dolphins. I had an incredible buzz from it, and a smile that lasted for days. It was something that I had wanted to do for years so I was really happy and it had a big impact on me.

I then started to fantasize about running a swimming with dolphins business – not one that took three trips a day but one that would be more about people immersing themselves in the dolphins' world for a week at a time and using the experience to help them gain perspective and stimulus for any issues they wanted to crack in their lives.

I visualized it intensely. I researched companies in New Zealand that ran these trips. I carried a picture in my wallet of my dolphin trip. I went on another trip in the Bahamas. I was on a dolphin trip mailing list. I kept talking to people about my dream. Every day I found myself experiencing bizarre coincidences. I met people who had some kind of connection to dolphins. By chance I met two people who facilitate dolphin trips. I also met somebody so inspired by the idea of people using nature as a stimulus to help them have ideas about their lives, that she set up a business that did just that, The Big Stretch. She in turn inspired me to believe I could do it with dolphins. When I opened newspapers I kept on finding articles that were relevant. Just walking down the street was giving me ideas as my mind was spotting useful stimuli and making creative connections.

Eventually, with so much energy behind the idea, I set up Mypod Ltd with my good friend Dido; a business that is all about taking people out of their work environments and giving them the time, space and the best stimulus the world can provide so they can make the changes they want in their lives. A true articulation of all that we do at **?What If!** and a great complement to the work that I do on business creativity.

A part of me likes to think that the universe was colluding to support me in getting a breakthrough. I believe that the energy we send out, we get back. However, what I was experiencing as coincidence could also be explained by my attunement to the issue and my heightened awareness of relevant stimulus. So, while the universe was colluding to help me, this was only because I asked it nicely and was listening to its answers.

hot plane

cheesy planet

MAKE IT IN YOUR FACE AND GET THE UNIVERSE TO WORK FOR YOU!

you are here!

DOING IT ✓

Get creative. Think of how you can represent your particular opportunity or objective and any ideas that you have. You can use pictures, symbols, music, books, video, clothing, furniture, Wiccan rituals – whatever brings it to life and can be placed where you hang out. If you want to get fit, carry pictures of healthy people with you in your wallet, put them on your fridge and on your mirror. Take out your sexiest clothes and hang them on the wall in your house. Make a scrapbook of all the things you want to do and the way you will feel when you are fit and spend at least 10 minutes a day looking at it. Just get any symbols that give you the feeling you are going for and make it In Your Face by putting them around your home, at work, in your pockets, as bookmarks – anywhere that you will see, feel, touch, smell, taste them regularly. Opportunities for you to realize your ambition will soon start showing up; ideas will flow and so much energy will build towards your objective, that it will become hard to do anything else but succeed.

FIFTH BIT:

IDEAS

IT'S IDEAS TIME

CAPTURE YOUR OPPORTUNITY!

When you have done the Insight Exercises in the previous section, you will have a clearer view as to what the specific issue is that you want to crack. Although this may change as you have ideas and ponder it further, for the moment write it down and put it up on your wall. Now you know what you're going for!

BEWARE OF THE BRAIN TRAP!

Our brains are fabulous learning machines. When we have an experience our brain files it away in case it is useful in the future. When we have a challenge that looks similar to what we have experienced before, our brain goes straight back to what we did last time and provides us with a tried and tested solution.

This is an incredibly fast and efficient way to live and learn. For instance, if I put my hand into a fire one day and burn it, if on the following day I saw another fire that wasn't the same but looked familiar … you get the picture.

Through this process we learn and we grow. While this process is great for our development

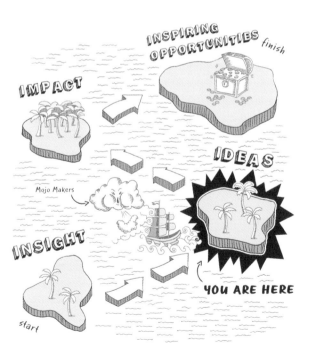

INSPIRING OPPORTUNITIES *finish*

IMPACT

Mojo Makers

IDEAS

INSIGHT

YOU ARE HERE

start

THE MORE
OFTEN YOU DO
SOMETHING
THE HARDER IT
IS TO DO IT
DIFFERENTLY

as human beings, it is very bad for creativity because whenever an opportunity arises for us to be creative, our brain does quite the opposite. It looks to see what we have done before. In short, we are hard-wired not to be creative.

Imagine that you have spent the last 10 years of your life reviewing people. You have been on courses teaching you how to do it and must have done it 500 times by now. You believe that you understand the best way to do it and are happy with your results. Not only are you lacking motivation to try something new, but with all that experience it's really hard to think of how it could be done. Your brain will automatically reference everything that you have done before and get caught up in your past experience.

A friend of mine was once taught to bake a traditional family cake by her mother. Once it was baked her mother cut the two ends off the cake and threw them in the bin. Intrigued by this, she asked her mom why she had done it. Her response was that she had been taught to bake this cake in this way and therefore that was how she had always done it. So my friend phoned up her grandmother and asked why she had taught her mom to bake like this – surely there was some fabulous family secret. Her grandmother explained that she did it because her baking tray was bigger than her cake tin, so the cake wouldn't fit in. And that's the way it works. We always do what we have done before. We are programmed to.

To make matters worse, the more experience we gain on a particular issue – say, reviewing a team – the harder it is to be creative when doing it. More experience means that the hard-wiring gets more and more embedded and therefore it becomes harder and harder to break out of a pattern of thinking. In fact, the more expert you become on a subject, the more rigid your thinking becomes.

The opposite is the case with children. They have relatively little past experience and therefore find it perfectly natural to invent 20 ways to use a cardboard box. 'It's a spaceship, a fort, a place for spies to plan secret missions, it's a toilet … oops' But as adults we just classify a cardboard box as 'packaging' because we have seen it before and know what it does.

So, as we mature and enjoy rich experiences in our lives, our brains become more programmed with past experience and consequently we find it harder to have new and different ideas. To break out of this backwards thinking we need to stimulate our imagination.

Some stimulus can cause profound reactions whilst others create an impact that is much more subtle. You don't really know until you try, so playing with stimulus is experimental and is best done in a playful frame of mind. Some you win, some you lose. If you don't get new and different ideas, just try something else. Stimulus should create energy and engage you. If they don't, you are either not being playful enough or it's simply not stimulating – so move on! Simple examples of stimulus include writing your opportunity or challenge in a different way or learning how someone else has faced a similar issue.

While there are thousands of types of stimulus, they can be grouped under five main principles:

1. Re-expression

2. Related worlds

3. Revolution

4. Random links

5. Relax

(These principles are covered in more depth in the fabulous book *Sticky Wisdom*. But for now, pages 166–82 are a summary.)

STIMULUS IS ANYTHING THAT CAUSES A REACTION IN US

RE-EXPRESSION

Perspective is everything! How happy we are, how we live our lives, how successful we feel, all comes from our perspective – as does getting stuck or achieving breakthroughs. There are many ways that you can re-express an opportunity or issue that is concerning you.

SOME THINGS YOU CAN DO

The words we use give us a very rigid view of our issue. By using different words to describe our issue we look at it differently. (See the example on the opposite page.)

So by describing your issue in a different way, you will see it differently and will consequently have different ideas. Doing this before starting any creative process gives you fresh insights and angles on the matter in hand.

There are many ways to look at your issue differently. You could draw it, sculpt it, mime it, bake it, or you could look at it as if through someone else's eyes: a hobbit, Angelina Jolie, Ian Fleming, Christopher Columbus, a pigeon, Neil Diamond. It doesn't matter what the angle is, as long as it changes your perspective and helps you create new and different ideas.

Some of my favorites are featured later in the book in a highly 'do-able' form:

• Splurge Time

• Back to the Future

• My Clever Friends

• Go Visual

• Through a Child's Eyes

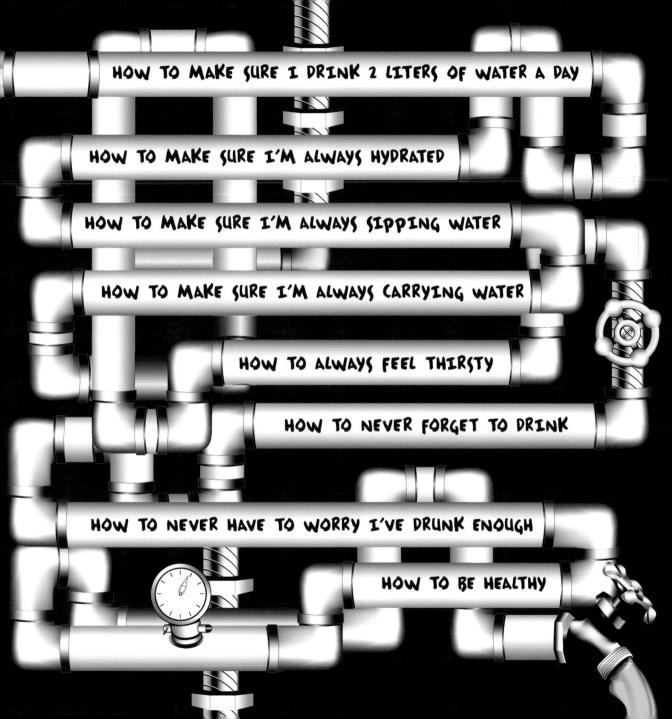

RAC – BREAKDOWNS ARE BUSTED

The breakdown and recovery market is under pressure. There is intense competition and cars are more reliable than ever, so there are fewer breakdowns needing such a service. Drivers also don't like the idea of breaking down, it has such negative connotations as it means something has gone wrong.

By changing perspective, we re-expressed their business goal as 'keeping drivers on the road'. This re-expression lead to the idea of RAC Solutions featuring a 28-point preventative car check and no call-out discount. The aim of the idea is to keep motorists on the road and avoid breakdowns. Launched in 2003, it scored a 96% positive rating on a customer opinion survey, resulted in an increase in revenue per customer, drove a reduction in new member recruitment costs and led to a more empowered workforce.

RAC Solutions broke them out of the breakdown business and into the Driving Reassurance business.

RELATED WORLDS

No matter what your issue is, you can be sure that it has been solved before! It won't necessarily have been in precisely the same context, but the essence of the issue will be the same.

Related Worlds is the simple process of using the solutions that have worked before. The example on the right explores the question of how you become more brave. To get maximum effect from stimulus, bring the issue to life as best you can. For example, if you want to understand how people become more brave in the army you could:

- Imagine being in the army (a bit weak unless you're ex-SAS)
- Go paintballing (a bit of 'acting as if' goes a long way)
- Watch *Platoon* or a similar film (but remember what you're looking for)
- Go talk to a real-life soldier (wow, a proper hero, that's stimulus!)

The more you bring it to life, the better you engage. The better you engage, the better your ideas!

At **?What If!** we often use Naïve Experts. They are experts in the opportunity we want to crack, but we don't tell them the context of the issue in question, so they stay naïve. If we didn't keep them in the dark, they would start to advise us instead of providing pure stimulus.

In the case of 'How to become more brave?' we got a Staff Sergeant from an airborne division to come and tell us how he encourages bravery. He talked about how guns are used to get soldiers out of trouble. The business which we were working with adapted that principle to issuing their people with 'I've screwed up' cards. They got two cards at the start of every year and if things went wrong they could play the card to make sure there were no repercussions. To further reinforce the idea, at their annual reviews, if they hadn't used them, their boss wanted to know why. Nice.

HOW DO I BECOME MORE BRAVE?

First, be clear on what it is you want to do
'How do I become more brave?'

Ask, 'Where in the world do people become more brave?'
The armed forces, extreme sports, stand-up comics, bullfighters, kids going to the dentist.

Ask, 'What do they do to become more brave?'
Join the armed forces. Take small steps and develop bravery over time. Create camaraderie for support, practice lots and sometimes get it wrong.

Ask 'How can I apply that to my life?'
Join a circus skills class where you can learn basic skills first with a group of people in a safe environment. At the end of the course arrange a performance. If you feel more confident as a result, apply some of the principles to other areas of your life that need a boost. For instance, public speaking, dancing, making love.

NIKE GETS STIMULATED

When Nike wanted to crack 'how to mobilize London behind the Nike brand', they got creative. One of my friends from Nike had just been trained by **?What If!** and had learnt how to use stimulus, so she ran a creative session using all sorts of exercises. As they were particularly interested in engaging large numbers of people behind the brand they asked: 'Where else in the world do lots of people get motivated and impassioned behind a movement?'

They came up with religion, sport, fashions and … cults. Their stimulus became a leading expert on cults, talking about how they get so many people devoted to a cause. Now Nike didn't want to start a cult, but they did want a cult following, people who felt that the brand had a positive impact in their lives.

By applying the principles that they learnt from this expert they came up with starting ideas for a promotional event, its communication strategy and how to engage huge numbers of people behind it. It has been so successful it has been replicated in many countries around the world and usually is oversubscribed in days. Nike, you rock!

EXPLODING TOILETS

At **?What If!** we have worked on more toilet cleaning projects than your average creative hotshop. After a while you have to search harder for inspiration on how to come up with something new and different.

One of our inventors was on vacation in a remote part of the world when he noticed a rather unusual toilet ritual. Locals would dig a hole, line it with leaves and twigs, 'do the do' then cover it with petrol and set light to it. They then cover it and it explodes leaving no evidence at all.

The principles were interesting. There was a bang that signals something powerful has happened. There is a change of format – the 'do' is transformed. So they applied this to the issue and came up with a toilet cleaner that fizzes when dropped in the toilet. It then changes color to let you know that something has happened. The result – sparkly toilets everywhere and people are satisfied with their cleaning power.

THE MOST INSIDIOUS OF RULES ARE THE ONES THAT AREN'T RULES AT ALL

THEY ARE THE
LIMITATIONS
THAT WE
INVENT FOR
OURSELVES

NAUGHTY STRIPPERS

In Boise, Idaho, total nudity was banned in public unless for 'serious artistic merit', thus making strip clubs cover up. However, one strip club, Erotic City, managed to break the rules. They asked the simple but powerful question: 'What if gentlemen coming to watch ladies taking all their clothes off had some serious artistic merit? In what circumstances could that happen?'

This question unlocked a cracking solution that kept them on the right side of the law. On entering said establishment, clients purchased a sketch pad and pencil for $15, and so 'Art Nights' were born and on those nights G strings were removed with abandon. While I can only imagine some of those etchings, I say hoorah for creativity. Once again self-expression blossomed.

REVOLUTION

Our thinking is restricted by the rules and constraints that we have learned in our lives or assumed for this situation. But just like Erotic City, we too can break free. By breaking those rules we free up our thinking so that our ideas can be truly creative. The first stage is to write down the rules. Here's an example, using the statement 'I want to learn how to play the guitar.'

HERE ARE SOME RULES …	NOW LET'S BREAK THEM
You have to practice lots …	*'What if it was easy?'*
It's painful to begin with …	*'What if it sounded great from the start?'*
You need to have a guitar to practice …	*'What if you could practice without a guitar?'*
Guitars are big to carry around …	*'What if you always had your guitar with you?'*
You have to learn to play it …	*'What if the guitar could play itself?'*

Let's just choose one to demonstrate.
'What if the guitar could play itself?'

In what circumstances could that happen?
Maybe the guitar could show me where to put my fingers for different chords by lighting up. It could even be programmed to play certain tunes so that I could learn by following the lights and not have to worry about reading books. Sounds a bit *Star Trek* to you – well not to the folks at Yamaha! They've done just that.

Don't worry about judging the idea, see how the process works. What ideas could you get from the other four rules? There are a few provocative examples in this book, but feel free to make up your own.

SAUCY THINKING

Here's one from Heinz ketchup:

'Ketchup takes ages to pour.'

'What if we could make it pour quickly?'
'What if that was what made it special?'
'What if you didn't have to pour it?'

The Heinz team then asked the all-important question:

In What Circumstances Could That Happen?
Their advertising agency came up with the idea of making the slow pouring a virtue which they did in their successful ad campaign. Since then of course, they have invented formats where you don't have to pour the ketchup, you just squeeze the bottle. Simple stuff, great ideas.

You can play with Revolution in the Big Questions section later (see pages 202–3).

WORLDWIDE CORRIE

I travel constantly. I watch very little TV largely because my time is in demand but also because I find it difficult to watch anything regularly; so when the whole world was raving about watching the program *24* I had never caught an episode.

What if I could watch my favorite program no matter where I was?

I discovered that Slingbox have found a way to stream that special program through the Internet, allowing you to pick it up in the same way you pick up your emails. So it allows you to transfer any channel that you can get on cable to your PC anywhere in the world. No matter if you are in Beijing or Belgrade, Boston or Bermuda, from now on you never have to miss an episode of *Coronation Street* or that big game.

RANDOM LINKS

Any stimulus can give you great ideas. The most creative people I know regularly use the world around them to give them great new thinking. Anyone can do it – you just need to be playful and in a state that lets your mind wander down fresh avenues of thought and creativity.

You also need some random stimulus.

Fortunately we are all surrounded by it constantly. Open a magazine and what's the first thing you see? Let your radio search out a new station, what music is being played? Call a friend and ask them to tell you what they can see in front of them.

HERE IS HOW USING RANDOM LINKS WORKS

Write down your issue	'How to get more freshness in my life?'
Get some random stimulus	A toothbrush.
Explore the stimulus, what does it make you think?	I use it twice a day. It's a habit. It's the same time every day. It reminds me to floss too. It's flexible. It wears out in months. Toothbrush design is always changing.

Sophie, a good friend of mine, always carries a box of postcards with her just in case she needs a creative boost; she is never stuck for ideas (and is great at staying in touch with family and friends).

Now ask:

'So what ideas does this give me?'

It might make you think that you have a habit of brushing your teeth, so where else do you have habits? Perhaps you have a habit of reading the Sunday papers so maybe what you should do is ask your newsagent to deliver you a random magazine and newspaper so you have a structure that guarantees something different arrives on your doorstep every week, thus breaking

your habit. This would probably become dull after a few months too, so then you'll need to come up with a new idea.

Simple, quick, effective. But remember, it only works if you are playful.

There are a couple of simple Random Links exercises later in the book.

- Bag of Tricks (see page 208)
- Open-top Bus (see page 210)

RELAX

While our brain has an incredible capacity to store and process information, much of that capacity is unavailable to us when we are in busy mode – talking on the phone, driving the car, listening to the radio or thinking about what we are going to have for dinner. However, when we relax and start to focus upon one thing, such as a piece of music, our breathing or a picture, we are able to access more of our brain, thus making more connections and having more creative ideas. In a relaxed state we are also able to remove the stress from our lives so we get a double hit of being more chilled and having fabulous ideas.

It has been said that we are human beings not human doings; well, this trick for having ideas is about being and not doing, and that just suits me fine – lazy as I am. Relaxation can take many forms. In each case, though, the key thing is that the mind slows down. Singular focus and repetitive actions can help achieve the right state, so although running, playing tennis and driving long distances don't necessarily sound relaxing, they can be relaxing for your brain. Salvador Dali and Thomas Edison used to just nod off thinking about their ideas. Judging by their respective creative outputs, this simple technique clearly reaps great rewards.

TIME FOR THE MOJO!

The 5 Rs are principles for finding stimulus. They are intended as a guide for you to invent your own exercises that will help you to generate new and creative ideas. Shortly, you can get stuck into some of my favorites, but before you get your hands dirty, remember, it's not the exercises, tools, games or techniques that are key to unlocking your genius.

> To get your mojo working you need to be in a playful state, and not worry about getting things 'right'.

I have worked with tens of thousands of people in helping them become more creative. However, I have noticed many different reactions in response to trying out a stimulus. One reaction is to have a ball, to get playful and just go with the flow. The other extreme reaction is to get self-conscious and analytical so the people in question just don't see it – they have no ideas and have an altogether terrible time. It's pretty obvious which group have the best ideas, but the key for this to happen is to avoid the 'I'm so serious and clever' trap. There are two reasons for getting caught in that trap.

First, we all have our own particular beliefs, values, needs, past experiences that we use to filter and process any given stimulus and event … and thank the Lord for that! This is why people are so varied and interesting. There is no right or wrong as to how we react to a given stimulus, just our own little special-ness. But it does mean that by involving people other than just yourself when searching for creative solutions to a certain issue, you will naturally get more varied ideas thus making the process richer, giving you a better chance of finding a successful outcome.

Secondly, the way that we are at any given point – our state – has a huge effect on the way we engage in creativity. In order to engage with stimulus and allow it to give you ideas, you must be sensitive and open to where it may take you. In the 21st century, we are surrounded by more stimulus than ever before – TV, books, billboards, people, cars, lights, music, action … it's a constant bombardment from when we wake up in the morning to when we go to sleep. You might think that this would mean that we are surrounded by masses of great ideas, but this is clearly not the case.

In fact, the problem is that most of us are over-stimulated, with our conscious brains even busier and noisier than ever before. The result of this over-stimulation is that we have become numb to what is going on around us and unaware of the reactions that show up in our state. People crave a little peace in their lives so their heads can focus and slow down. This is why so many people create their own personal havens. They listen to iPods, escape to the country, take up yoga – all ways of shutting out the outside world. People are creating personal sanctuaries and it's hardly surprising.

Clearly, then, before using any stimulus tool or technique the single most important thing to do is get in the right state.

- Find somewhere with few distractions where you won't get interrupted.

- Take a few deep breaths and connect with your state. How are you feeling?

- Is there anything you need to do to get into the right state? Have a stretch, drink some water, make a call? If so, do it now!

This next section of the book is a practical one. It contains numerous exercises that will help you come up with fabulous ideas to help you become energized and get moving. It is by no means exhaustive. Also, please feel free to adapt the exercises, invent new ones, or rip them apart and start again. My vision is that this chapter grows and grows over the years with other peoples' favorite provocations and exercises, so please do experiment. The best stimulus produces the most ideas, so don't worry about the process: if you're having ideas, don't stop, just keep going.

MOJO MAKING!

Before each exercise take a deep breath and check in with where you are. Are you playful enough to invent 20 things that you can do with your underwear right now?

How is your state? Mine often needs a bit of buffing up before starting any creative exercises.

You can do this in any number of ways. For instance, try this simple visualization:

1. Stand up and take three deep breaths.

2. Picture in your mind's eye a time when you were having fun and lots of ideas. It can be any time at all – with friends over a drink, with your family, in the office, on vacation, whatever. All it takes is for it to be a time you were enjoying yourself and loving the flow of ideas.

3. Now imagine yourself in your body looking out through your eyes. Notice how it feels to be creative and playful. Feel the vitality of your body. Notice the clarity of your thinking. What emotions do you feel? Enjoy how connected you are.

4. When your creativity and cheekiness feel 'strong like a bull', you are ready to play.

REASONS TO BE CHEERFUL

If you are still not quite in the right state, this exercise never fails.

What is it?

A simple, reframing exercise. It is fast and effective and can also be used for when you just need a boost.

Why it's good

When we are stuck, we spend a lot of time focusing on the 'stuckness', which can become all-consuming in itself. This exercise reminds us of fabulous things in our lives and this puts the stuckness into perspective. As a result, this will make us feel energized, resourceful and full of the joys of spring, raring to go in the knowledge that this could be the dawning of your new future.

DOING IT ✓

1. Stand up, take a deep breath and feel strong/the force (depending on what works for you).

2. Write a list of why your life is so fantastic right now!

3. Write quickly and with passion – enjoy.

4. Don't censor, just write and think of examples from all aspects of your life.

5. Stop, breathe and relax. Read back through your list. How do you feel?

SPLURGE TIME

What is it

Describing your opportunity in lots of different ways. A big uncensored stream of consciousness. A creative scrawl.

Why it's good

We often get trapped into seeing our issue in just one way. By shifting our perspective, we see the issue differently and are able to come up with creative solutions.

DOING IT ✓

Write down your issue in 10, 20, even 30 different ways. The trick to making this work is to do it VERY QUICKLY. If you think about it too much your conscious brain takes control and you lose a little drop of genius. There is no right or wrong, so get scrawling. Use words you have never used before.

Make some up. Be descriptive. What else is it like? How about some metaphors? Don't stop until your hand goes numb or it's time for bed.

Here's One From My Life

I often spend too much time away from home, working, and I tend to work many hours when I'm not away.

My Issue: *How to get more work–life balance?*

- 'How to spend more time at home?'
- 'How to be healthier?'
- 'How to be less stressed?'
- 'How to learn how to switch off from work?'
- 'How to learn to relax?'
- 'How to leave my work behind?'
- 'How to learn to focus?'
- 'How always to be a good husband?'
- 'How to make work like play?'
- 'How to take life less seriously?'
- 'How to make the time count while I am with my family?'
- 'How to do only what matters to me?'

- 'How to live a life that makes me proud?'
- 'How always to keep growing?'
- 'How to learn a new thing every day?'
- 'How to be a sponge soaking up life's experience?'

  (That took 2 minutes 18 seconds!)

nice list, Chris - but
  how does it help?

When I look back at my list I notice that certain expressions cause more of a reaction in me – that is, my state changes more. I thought that my issue was all about work-life balance but the three areas that seem to resonate are:

1. Switching off from work.
2. Having a more fun attitude.
3. Always learning and growing.

The words we use make a huge impact on the ideas we have. In my case, it was worth my writing these in another 10 different ways to see if that generated any new perspectives.

EXAMPLE: 'SWITCHING OFF'

'Switching off from work' made me focus upon the word *'switch'*. I associate work with my mobile phone and my email.

When I walk into my home I now turn off my mobile and email and hide any electronic, worky equipment in a cupboard until the morning. If my wife Anna sees me using it out of work hours, then I have to listen to her favorite radio station for all the next week (hell on a stick!). When I go to work, I then kiss my wife, take out my worky gizmos again and focus on the day.

Simple, effective, do-able. Don't stop at one idea, keep writing Re-expressions until you have loads.

189

BACK TO THE FUTURE

What is it?

A powerful perspective shift that can create huge energy and clarity with regard to your issue or opportunity. You get advice and ideas from an older you and a younger you.

Why it's good

We often get trapped in our situation so that we lose perspective. Purely by remembering what is important and what makes a difference, we can get unleashed. Few perspectives are as powerful as those from near the beginning and near the end of your life.

DOING IT ✔

You can do this by visualizing a conversation, but personally I find it works great by writing yourself a letter – one from the future and one from the past.

Seat yourself somewhere comfortable and quiet. Imagine yourself to be much older and in the twilight of your years with most of your life lived. Now write a letter to you in the present time. This is a letter of advice, of perspective. Write whatever comes to you, whatever seems important. Don't censor yourself, just write. It really helps to imagine how you will be by that time, what you have experienced and what you have learnt. When it feels complete sign off and put it in an envelope for the present you. Take the letter into another room, pour yourself a cup of tea and read it. What ideas does this letter give you?

Now kneel on the floor and write the letter from you as a child using the hand you don't usually write with. Colored crayons can really bring this to life. Again, don't edit yourself, but write from your heart, write from the younger you. Think about what is important to you as a child, what you love, what makes you tick. When you're finished, hang out for a while, play a game, have some fun – you deserve it. Then change rooms, pour yourself a cup of juice and read your letter …

MY CLEVER FRIENDS

What is it?

Imagining what somebody else might do in your situation.

Why it's good

By creating other perspectives on the opportunity, you can often see ways to create ideas to make the most of the opportunity.

DOING IT ✓

Think of someone who is a bit special. Someone you admire or maybe someone who really pisses you off. The key thing is that they create some kind of impact in the world and stand for something, be it a way of life, a belief or a personality trait. For example, Dennis Hopper, Mahatma Gandhi, Eric Morecambe, Flash Gordon, Princess Diana, Felicity Kendal, your Grandad …

Now imagine their life, what is important to them, what they stand for, what it is you admire about them.

- What would they do in your situation?
- What advice would they give you?
- How would they get unstuck?
- In what way would they make this opportunity happen?

CALL A FRIEND!

Recently a friend of mine was stuck in one of those meetings where the discussion was going nowhere. People were being far too analytical and as a result it looked like they could go on for weeks without seeing a glimmer of a proposal. At that point, he asked himself, 'Who do I know who would be fabulous in this situation?' The answer came to him – Daz!

The next question was, 'So what would he do if he was here now?' The solution was obvious: Daz was a no-nonsense straight-talker and would have jumped in and put his cards on the table. So that's exactly what my mate did. He stopped the meeting, shared his observations and suggested a new way forward. Everyone was hugely relieved. They had all been thinking the same thing but didn't know what to do. Nor did my mate, but he had a friend who did!

GO VISUAL

What is it?

Capturing your issue or opportunity without using words. You can get a bit artistic and draw or paint it. You can make collages with pictures from magazines. You can sculpt, whittle, mosaic, craft, weave, knit a representation. Whatever works for you.

Why it's good

Creating visuals means that you use your brain in a different manner to when you are using words, so by doing some finger painting you will actually think in new ways. Once you have made visuals of the concern in hand, you will have much more space to go creative in your interpretation of what the issue is and how you may be able to tackle it. It's a bit like art. Everybody sees something different in it, and the longer you look and change your perspective on it, the more ideas you get. We often get people to draw their issue or make a Lego® model of it and then ask other people with no connection to it to interpret it first.

Often it can bring fabulous insights. Equally, if you interpret your own sketch by just blurting stuff out then you will find that your perceptions will become richer and more fertile.

DOING IT ✓

So what do you see?

Get playful, get a big piece of paper and let fly. This is not about being artistic, but about having fun – you can make sense of it all later. Mrs. Simpson from class 3B won't be judging your efforts, so let yourself go! Who knows, you might create some art!

When you look at it, what does it make you think, what ideas does it give you? How else could you interpret it? If you turn it upside down, what relevance does that have to your opportunity? What ideas does that give you?

QUICK SKETCH SOLUTION

We were once called in to help a footwear business with an internal communication issue to do with establishing the direction of the business.

The board were having all sorts of problems and decided enough was enough, they needed outside help. After listening to the board explaining their issue for half an hour or so, we felt no closer to the solution. We had to try something else or it was going to be a very long day.

We asked them to draw the issue. One of the six board members drew this.

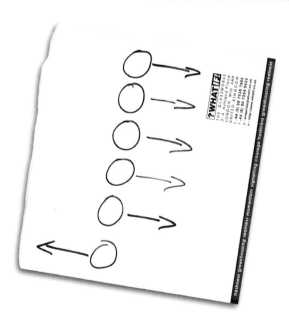

After a little exploration it became obvious that the issue was not communication, it was alignment. One of the six was interpreting the vision of the business very differently to the others. Once this was realized the solution was simple. They just had to get clear on where they were going and what each of them had to do to achieve it.

So get your crayons out.

THROUGH A CHILD'S EYES

What is it?

A simple exercise that creates a very different perspective – that of a child.

Why it's good

Every experience we have influences the way we think and create ideas. By the time we become adults, these experiences can overcomplicate situations and filter our reactions to stimulus, but a child reacts very differently to the world. Things are simple. They are good or bad, fun or dull. A child's curiosity and imagination are rampant. By seeing the world through a child's eyes, you often find simple solutions to your issue, because the whole issue changes.

DOING IT ✓

Firstly, take a few breaths and close your eyes. As you relax, notice how your mind becomes more clear. Now imagine that you are a child – choose an age when you were playful, imaginative and curious. The more relaxed and cheeky you become, the easier it is to have great ideas.

Remember what it was like to be you at that time. There is only now. You focus upon one thing at a time. You don't censor your thinking or your actions. Things are simple. The strangest things grab your imagination. A simple game can last all morning. Hang out there for a while and remember all the things that are important to you.

Now, describe your issue from this perspective:

• What is it?
• Why are you stuck?
• What are the things standing in your way?

To help you get into character, I recommend doing this standing up and throwing a ball around or kneeling on the floor playing with a toy or going outside and kicking leaves.

PHONE A FRIEND

What is it?
A conversation between you and a friend about an opportunity or issue you have.

Why it's good
The simple act of verbalizing your concern and explaining it to somebody else will often help you find a new perspective, idea or solution. Women seem to have a natural ability to do this in a way that men often struggle with; they have used it for years and now us men are in on the secret.

Friends can give you a different angle on the situation and help you create inspiring solutions. Two heads are better than one when it comes to ideas. Talking to others about your opportunity can often add energy to getting it solved, therefore creating movement. Sometimes talking about it puts it in perspective and your concern just becomes less important.

DOING IT ✓

As the saying goes: 'A problem shared is a problem halved.' Blurt it out, notice how it feels, then listen, then chat some more … You can do this freestyling or resort to the more structured Blurt it Out (see page 140).

bla bla bla bla bla bl
words words
talk talk talk
more words bla bla
RUBBISH
LIES DECEPTION
FAKE
NONESENSE
PRETENTION
good stuff
HONESTY
TRUTHFULNESS
AUTHENTIC

'CHILDREN ALWAYS UNDERSTAND.
THEY HAVE OPEN MINDS.
THEY HAVE BUILT-IN
BULLSHIT DETECTORS.'

MADONNA

WHERE ELSE IN THE WORLD?

What is it?

Thomas Edison once said that your idea only needs to be original in its adaptation to your problem. In other words, find out who has had the same problem, see what they have done and copy the solution. We have already done this one earlier in the book when we learnt from the army how to become more brave (see pages 170–71).

Why it's good

This is a fast and simple technique because no matter what your issue or concern, someone else has had it before. It also allows you to get creative stimulus from particular worlds that you have access to or are especially interested in.

DOING IT ✓

- Write your issue down.
- Ask where in sport has someone faced a similar issue.
- In which film did such a situation exist?
- Who in the world is an expert at overcoming such an issue?
- Where in business have people solved this problem?
- When have you experienced a similar issue in another aspect of your life?
- When has nature faced this issue?
- Who does this every day of their life?
- Which of your friends have had a similar headache?

Then explore the principles behind their success and apply them to your issue. If you get too thinky thinky, just Splurge and do it again (see page 188). If you think widely enough you will always have somewhere to look for inspiration. Remember to bring it to life in as real a way as possible so you can fully engage with the stimulus.

BE CREATIVE – IT'S THE LAW!

We were once working with the government on a fabulous project: how to help judges make the most of their time? One of the issues that came up was that lawyers don't always present their cases in a straightforward way, so judges spend a lot of time unravelling arguments and understanding cases.

We asked where else in the world do people do everything they can to cut down on wasting time? One place we thought of was with racing cars, so we brought in a designer to talk to us. He explained how through technical design you can cut down the wind resistance that a car experiences.

This gave us the idea of giving incentives to lawyers to help judges go faster and cut down their daily resistance. Now British judges will nominate lawyers for awards when they demonstrate effective use of court time. They are the court's version of the Oscars and give lawyers public recognition which should help them find clients and build their business. Thus the judges become more effective, more baddies get locked up and once again Britain becomes the bastion of civilized society. Bravo for innovation!

BIG QUESTIONS

What is it?

Throughout my life whenever I have become stuck, wise and clever people have popped up and helped get me moving again. I was fortunate to have met them and fortunate that they knew what questions to ask to help me see things differently.

For years I spent my time devoted to 'improving myself'. It was a never-ending battle. I would complete the next qualification/seminar/book, only to realize that there was something more urgent/burning/tricky to deal with. Then one day, my fabulous friend and coach Tony, asked 'When will you have done enough to be happy with who you are?'

It was a big question and it immediately jolted me out of the ridiculous pattern I had become caught up in. I knew that if I carried on this way, I would never be satisfied. I would always feel the desire to be more insightful, attuned, aware, fit, spiritual, talented. In an instant I knew that I had forgotten that we are all whole already. My focus needed to be more about remembering this wholeness and pursuing self-discovery, rather than the very dull self-improvement shenanigans I'd got bogged down in.

With big questions you always carry a guru sage in your pocket.

Why it's good

The right question is the keystone. Ask it and all the difficulty and stuckness falls crashing to the ground and once again clarity prevails. Choosing the right question from the thousands of potentials is down to intuition. So if in doubt, ask more questions.

At **?What If!** we always found it hard to find great people who can come into the business and make an impact fast. So the Big Question we asked was 'How can we get great people dying to join us?' Some of the solutions were to make **?What If!** the best place to work in

Europe, to make work exciting and high profile and to hold *Pop Idol-* or *X Factor*-type auditions so there is more fun and stretch in the recruitment process.

DOING IT ✓

Ask yourself:

- *'What if I couldn't fail? What would I do then?'*

- *'What if I had only one day to live? What would I do then?'*

- *'What if I had all the money in the world? What would I do then?'*

- *'What if I was trying to get fired? What ideas come to mind?'*

- *'What if it was my son or daughter who was stuck and frustrated? What advice would I give them?'*

- *'What if my life had to be exceptional or I would be sent to jail?'*

- *'What if I wasn't scared of anything?'*

- *'What if I wanted to be famous?'*

- *'What if learning and growing were the most important things in my life? Then what would I do?'*

- *'What if I wasn't stuck at all and I've had the answer all along?'*

WHAT IF CLOTHES FIT PERFECTLY EVERY TIME?

We've all got clothes that fit fabulously, flatter our physiques and therefore are worn constantly. Finding them in the first place, however, can be a painfully hit-and-miss affair.

Intellifit, the US-based award-winning creator of the Intellifit System body scanner, has come up with a really creative solution. Using low-power radio waves to map the body's measurements through your clothing, Intellifit's body scanners can size you up in around 10 seconds. You can then use the Find What Fits search engine kiosk to find tailor-made clothes, so guaranteeing the fit that you want every time. The system is being trialled in a number of malls and stores this year and already looks like being a winner. Say good-bye to the fitting room and hello to Intellifit.

THE GRASS IS NOT ALWAYS GREENER ON THE OTHER SIDE!

Lucy, one of my top buddies, was presented with the disturbing fact that her husband, Luke, was madly in love with someone else. He is a passionate, romantic type and felt that he had no choice but to spend time with this new woman – even though he was clear that he didn't want to leave his family.

Lucy's instinctive and emotional response was to insist that Luke stopped this affair immediately (can't blame her for that) but at the same time she knew that if she would do so it would make the affair even more desirable. So she used Revolution to come up with another solution.

'What if instead of trying to keep them apart, I tried to force them together?' Now that may sound a little reckless, but that was exactly what she did. She hired them a small place near where she lived, allowed Luke total access to his children and the family home from which he worked and encouraged him to spend as much time with his new girlfriend as he could in order to see if she was really who he wanted.

After looking at family life from outside the fold, Luke got a very different perspective and came to realize that the grass wasn't greener after all. The result was that Lucy and Luke are now back together and using this experience as a catalyst to rejuvenate their 14-year relationship.

Now *that's* a revolution.

BAG, STEAL OR BORROW?

A whopping 94 percent of Japanese women in their 20s own a Louis Vuitton bag, and 92 percent a Gucci one. The numbers are lower in Europe and the States – but the craving for the latest look is just as strong. The problem is that few can actually afford a luxury bag, let alone keep up with the new fashion styles that are introduced each season.

But what if anybody could afford to have this season's bag? The internet company Bag, Steal or Borrow has come up with a creative solution. Their members are able to borrow the very latest designs, keeping them for as long as they want and then returning them when it is time for something new. And if they just can't bear to part with their favorite bag, then there is an option to buy as well. With a minimum commitment of three months, in the UK there are three levels of membership – Fashion Fabulous, Chic Boutique and Handbag Heaven – each offering a different degree of designer decadence. Now, fashionistas the world over will never have to experience accessory anxiety again.

BAG OF TRICKS

What is it?
A random links exercise for when you don't have the time to go hunting for ideas.

Why it's good
It's fast, simple, takes very little planning and creates a playful energy if you do it with mates.

DOING IT ✓

Ask a friend to fill a bag with random objects. Anything at all! A tennis ball, a picture of a donkey, phoney dog poo, fake snow, binoculars. Health and Safety would advise against broken glass, serrated knives, bear traps, etc. Just nice stuff.

You then focus upon your issue, pull out an object at random and explore it. Let your mind wander and see what ideas it gives you.

NO PIECE OF STIMULUS IS MORE THAN 6 DEGREES OF SEPARATION AWAY FROM A GREAT IDEA. YOU JUST HAVE TO WANT IT! BADLY!

SUCKING IT IN

During production of the Ballbarrow, entrepreneur James Dyson noticed that the filter in the spray-finishing room at his factory kept getting clogged up with particles. This was a very similar problem to that which he had experienced while using his traditional upright Junior Hoover at home, with both cloth and paper bags. As usual, James set about finding an answer to this problem.

He was inspired by a friend who told him that a nearby sawmill used a 'cyclone' to clear their air. Not having a clue what one was – but refusing to pay $150,000 to have one installed in his own factory – James decided he would make one of his own. He began by designing and constructing an industrial cyclone tower, which could exert forces of over 100,000 times the force of gravity. This spun the particles in the factory to the outside of the cyclone where they could be extracted and reused.

James knew by now that he also had an answer to the clogging vacuum cleaner. He spent the next three years in a workshop created from an old coach house near his home – and came out with the dual-cyclone cleaner, James Dyson's most successful invention ever.

OPEN-TOP BUS

What is it?

One of the easiest ways to get lots of random stimulus. All you have to do is get on a bus and open up your senses.

Why it's good

Cities have so much to see that we are largely blind to. We spend so much of our time focused on our feet, we rarely see the heavens. Open-top Bus helps you to see things from a different angle.

DOING IT ✓

Buy a ticket, get on the bus, go upstairs, soak it up. I find that doodling on a big pad of paper helps me bounce into ideas. The key to success is to make sure that you explore what grabs your attention and then apply it back to your issue and come up with ideas.

For instance:

How do I make sure I drink lots of water every day?

I see people running to get out of the rain.

People adapt their behavior to the change in weather. They have no choice.

How could I have no choice?

Watch vibrates to remind me. Only turns off when wet.

Take a pill that makes you thirsty for water every 20 minutes.

My body could tell me it's time to drink every 20 mins.

Intravenous hydration pack that automatically tops me up.

Employ water police who run round the office topping up glasses every 20 mins.

DAYDREAM BELIEVER

What is it?

Just letting your mind wander and seeing what comes up.

Why it's good

We access our subconscious regularly every day. Some clever people believe we spend more than 50 percent of our time in a dream-like state where we can access more of our creative genius. This technique simply increases the chances of a great output.

DOING IT ✓

First, focus on what the opportunity is. As you picture it in your mind's eye take a deep breath and relax. Now let the image drift away as you change your focus to the window and the world beyond or to the ceiling as you lie back on the sofa or to the candle as you soak in the bath.

Do whatever you do when you daydream the best. When you do come up with an idea, write it down, otherwise they tend to get lost somewhere in the ether beyond your window box.

DAYDREAMING IS NO LONGER A GUILTY PLEASURE, BUT AN ESSENTIAL CREATIVE TECHNIQUE

CHILL OUT

When Thomas Edison, one of the most prolific inventors of all time, had a problem to solve he used to sit on a tin tray with a stone between his knees and think about his issue. As he started to daydream, he would relax and get access to his subconscious. When he daydreamed too deeply and started to fall asleep, he would lose consciousness, drop the stone on to the tin and wake himself up. He would then start all over again, thus ensuring he had maximum daydream time.

One day Douglas Adams, author of *The Hitchhiker's Guide to the Galaxy*, lay down in a field after a few too many beers while on a trip to Holland. In his hand was his hitchhiker's guide to Europe, and as he relaxed staring up to the skies, inspiration hit him! By letting his mind wander freely and freshening up his creative juices, he combined the guide in his hand and the stars above and came up with the idea for his best-selling book.

YOUR MIND
STARTS
BEING
WHEN YOU
STOP
DOING

WALKING IN NATURE

What is it?

Getting physical surrounded by beauty. Most of my breakthrough moments have come to me when walking in nature, chatting to a friend.

Why it's good

Walking in nature is a double whammy for getting great ideas. Walking in itself helps you access your subconscious, so heightening the chances of a really cool idea.

Nature creates many and varied states in us while taking us on a sensory roller-coaster ride. Mountains, beaches, valleys, snow, grass, corn fields, rain, lakes, meadows, sun, beasties and birdies. They are always changing, always beyond our own creation.

Walking in nature works so well that a top pal of mine, Rosie, has set up a business that helps people do this in beautiful places with coaching as you walk. It's called The Big Stretch.

DOING IT ✔

From my experience, I find it takes a while to get into the state in which ideas start to flow – it's usually at least one hour. Chatting with a friend is great as the simple act of articulation helps us process the information differently, making lots of fresh creative connections.

Always carry a small note pad to capture the ideas. The idea for this book came to me whilst walking in Switzerland.

NATURE IS THE BEST SOURCE OF STIMULUS ON THIS PLANET

LET'S GET PHYSICAL

What is it?

Any activity that gets us out of our heads and into our bodies.

Why it's good

When our heads are busy, busy, busy we are usually using only our conscious brain. Physical (and repetitive) actions start to slow our brains down, so giving us access to more of our creative genius.

DOING IT ✓

It is key to think about what your issue is early in your activity so you can start to focus your brain's attention. Then all you have to do is let your mind drift as you get physical with whatever activity works for you. Here are some physical activities that people have told me work for them.

- Running
- Gardening
- Washing up
- Tennis
- Sailing
- Chopping logs
- Yoga
- Knitting
- Building a wall
- Skiing
- Painting
- Vacuuming
- Cycling
- Swimming

This list largely falls into two categories, so you can improve your home or get fit and have fabulous ideas at the same time.

Now that's creativity!

SLEEP ON IT

What is it?

This is the bit when you go to bed and close your eyes. It can also be in front of the TV on a Sunday afternoon or lying in the sun after a swim.

Why it's good

For centuries, inventors and innovators have used sleep as a way to gain inspiration and breakthrough thinking. In the course of going through our customary sleep patterns, we regularly engage with our subconscious, which makes connections even in our sleep. All you need to do is know how to use it.

DOING IT ✓

1. Begin to relax in bed and think gently about your opportunity. What I mean by gently is just to think about your opportunity or challenge in a neutral state. Don't get stressed out, simply acknowledge the issue with your head on the pillow. If you do get worked up by it, sleep can get tricky, and so does relaxing into the right state for you to access your subconscious. So take three deep breaths, think about it and chill.

2. Stop thinking about it, count sheep or whatever you do, relax and go to sleep.

3. When you wake up and are still in bed, write anything down that comes into your head. This must be done immediately or it will be forgotten as we do with most of our fabulous dreams. Even if it sounds surreal, write it down. This sends an important message to your brain that you need its input. Often the idea isn't perfectly formed, but needs developing.

4. Repeat night after night, catnap after catnap, until genius arises. It builds over time.

HOT BATH

What is it?

It's a big container for hot water. You fill it up and then you get in.

Why it's good

Most people find they have some of their best ideas when they are relaxing. To relax fully you need to work on your body as well as your mind. By lying in a hot bath, closing your eyes and chilling out, your whole state becomes receptive to having creative ideas.

People have been known to light candles. Now to all the guys out there, I don't want to push your sense of masculinity but a bathbomb could be your path to creative nirvana.

DOING IT ✓

- Soak, soak, chill
- Write down your ideas
- Now soak, soak, chill

And in the unlikely event of you not getting any ideas, at least you'll be clean! (We all like a clean 'un.)

PUB

What is it?
A fabulous network of rest and recuperation centres throughout the country.

Why it's good
The inspiration 'sweet spot' usually exists somewhere between the second and third pint when the banter is rising and yet the memory is still intact. The pub is good for relaxing you and taking away inhibitions. Although this technique has been proven to work fabulously for many years (see your average ad agency creative), I wouldn't recommend relying on it too heavily (see your average older ad agency creative).

DOING IT ✔

- Go to the pub with a good friend
- Buy a couple of pints, glasses of Chablis, tequila or soft drinks
- Chat about the issue
- Write down your thinking and ideas
- Come home before you say, 'What a genius idea. I'm throwing in my job right now.'

LAST BIT:

IMPACT

IMPACT

By now you have got some insight into your opportunity and have nailed what it is all about. You have also played with some exercises and generated ideas on how to make the most of it. It's now time to make some impact on your opportunity or challenge.

There are two stages to this:

1. Deciding which idea has the highest 'horn' factor – horn being excitement, passion and potential to create magic.

2. Making it happen.

The process of deciding can in itself be an incredibly informative exercise. Before getting stuck in, take a deep breath and notice how you feel.

- Nervous?
- Excited?
- Hungry?
- Confused?

Worry not, all is safe and well.

GETTING IT RIGHT OR GETTING IT WRONG

Some people avoid this moment as if it were a meeting with the Grim Reaper himself! By making a decision and making a commitment to do something, they worry that they may have got it wrong. They think that if they get it wrong, their life is ruined. Their friends will excommunicate them, their career is over and they will die alone in a ditch!

You may laugh, but you would be surprised how often people whip themselves into such a frenzy about the possibility of making a mistake that their busy protective minds start to make this kind of garbage up. (If your mind is still racing, go back to True or False – see page 150 – and carry out the exercise on what is going on in your mind right now.) But here's the news ... **There is no right or wrong.**

You have come up with creative solutions to making a part of your life abundant with opportunity. Some may work better than others but you will never really know unless you do them. Some may logically add up, but when you do them they don't work out at all! And vice versa!

Since you are doing something new that will affect your future there will naturally be a risk involved because you can't predict precisely what will happen. And there is always the risk that your ideas and solutions may create even more magic than you can handle.

Making decisions can be a bit like trying on clothes. Some clothes, even though they look great, just make you feel uncomfortable. Equally, there are others that when I see them on the rail I think, 'No way! Not me!', yet when I'm coerced into trying them on I fall instantly in love with them. Just like trying on clothes, you have to experiment with solutions and you have to be in the right mood or state.

LEAVES IN YOUR TEA CUP

No one can predict the future accurately every time. Otherwise I'd be betting a few bucks on the ponies. Intuition, however, can give us useful information. Sometimes, it just doesn't feel right to make a big change right now.

I have had experiences when logically I knew it was time to do something new, and yet my state and intuition told me not to rush it. I've often been very pleased that I listened.

By getting this far in the process, things will have changed for you already. All things change anyway, so if you wait long enough, a new opportunity will present itself. If you do make the decision to do nothing new, then make it consciously and commit yourself to reviewing your decision on a weekly basis. If you no longer need to change your life, you can accept it.

One of the major causes of distress in society today is not knowing what to accept and what to change. There are times that the status quo is right for now. The key thing is that if you truly do accept your current reality, you can only enjoy it.

Acceptance is a fabulous thing. It takes the pressure off and gives us time to smell the roses. It helps us go with the flow and stop fighting against what's happening. However, if there is still a part of you that is uncomfortable, and you have that Uncertain Feeling, it is time to make a change.

YOU MAKE THE PLAYS

When I was younger I was stuck. I felt paralyzed and couldn't move forward. My brother gave me the kick up the backside that I needed. His advice was:

MAKE A DECISION
NOW,
MAKE A PLAN
AND START IT.
IT'S JUST FOR NOW,
NOT FOR
THE REST OF YOUR LIFE.
IF YOU DON'T
LIKE IT
TOMORROW
~~START IT~~
~~CHOOSE~~
CHANGE IT!!

Simple, powerful, and true. Thanks, Mark!

So if you can genuinely accept your situation, with no distress, Bravo!
If not, it's time to make that change!

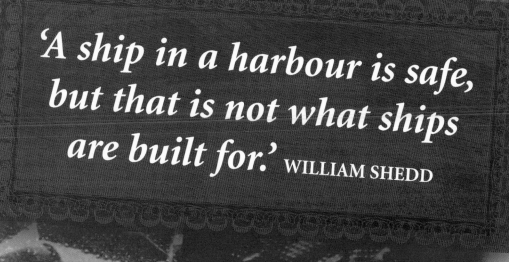

'A ship in a harbour is safe, but that is not what ships are built for.' WILLIAM SHEDD

Pull

CLEVER CLEVER THINKY THINKY

The Pros and Cons

Logic has its place in any decision. Sometimes it's enough to decide what to do. I know many people who write lists of pros and cons when making a choice. This can be very useful in quieting the mind. But it can also become a fast route to insanity.

I recently observed the conversation in my head as to whether I should cook or order in some Thai food. It was a farce and it carried on for over 10 minutes. There was always another reason why I should or I shouldn't. So a top tip for cutting through the crap is to limit it to five pros, five cons and to make sure they are True and not False.

For example:

- If I have a curry I'll eat too much – False
- If I eat too much I might not sleep
  so well – True
- I can choose to eat less – True
- I love Thai food – True
- Takeaways are a waste of money – False

Just order the damned food, Chris!

WHAT HAPPENS WHEN CLEVER CLEVER, THINKY THINKY DOESN'T WORK

When Takashi Hashiyama, president of Maspro Denkoh Corporation, had problems deciding which auction house should sell a $20m art collection, he had to turn away from logic.

He invited representatives from Sotheby's and Christie's to duel for the collection by playing rock, paper, scissors. Christie's won with scissors to Sotheby's paper. Mr. Hashiyama, told the *New York Times*: 'I sometimes use such methods when I cannot make a decision.'

MAKE IT REAL ...
THEN GET NAKED

Making things real is vital to any creativity. At **?What If!** we use this all the way through the innovation process to bring insights, stimulus and ideas to life. The advantages of doing so are enormous.

If I was to write an idea down on a piece of paper and show it to a friend or just tell them about it, they would only be able to engage with it at an intellectual level because it is only an intellectual concept. And the concept they have in their head may also be very different to mine – possibly a completely different idea!

But if I bring the idea to life in some way by drawing it, making a film about it or by leading them through a visualization, they will have the opportunity to engage with it in a fuller fashion. The idea becomes a sensory experience involving the whole person. By engaging with an idea in this way, you get a much truer reaction to the power of the idea and its strengths become immediately apparent.

Our Realness Studio people have a belief that if you make something Real, you have to Get Naked. They say that if you don't get the idea out, no one will know how big it is. And that's true. If you bring your idea to life you have to show it to people otherwise they can't engage with it, react to it and make it even better. This enables you to make a much more robust choice than by simply thinking it through. There are many ways to bring an idea to life, but before you do so you may need to flesh it out and fill in a bit more detail.

FUTURE PROOF

How do you get people to experience an event before it happens? This was a challenge put to us by one of our clients who needed to generate maximum impact for their Finlandia vodka brand from a single large event in Finland. The main event was to be a huge party in Finland that would raise awareness and communicate the unique purity of the Finlandia vodka brand, to be followed by a series of replicated smaller events in bars and clubs across the globe.

We brought the event to life by producing a 6-minute movie trailer vividly describing what the party would feel like, the sounds, smells, and projected visuals – crucially every point at which the vodka brand touched the consumer. Centered on the theme of the Finnish Midnight Sun we created a frozen forest, a glacial melting zone and a Midnight Sun arena. We also helped to create three iconic drinks that embodied the three zones. We formed a tight team of voiceover artists and animators, mixing their skills with live action to compress the whole 24-hour event into 6 minutes – all through the eyes of a party guest.

Only by sketching, storyboarding, acting out and scripting the event were we able to make it feel 'real' and absorbing. We had created a unique story for the brand, focusing on its pure ingredients and the Finnish landscape to give it worldwide appeal. The movie was used as the brief to the event team who recreated it faithfully in a forest in Lapland. The event took place in Lapland in June 2005 for 350 people from 35 countries – we even advised on where to buy the snow.

FILL IN THE GAPS

Before you can make any idea real you have to fill in the gaps. All too often people make a decision based upon a fantasized vision that bears little relation to reality. For instance, bizarre as it may seem, running a bar in Spain isn't all suntans and lounging by the pool.

So it's time for you to do a little research. This will be by no means exhaustive, but it will be enough to get you moving, either towards or away from the proposed solution. Your research could be as simple as:

- An hour on the Internet
- Phoning for advice
- Sending off for some information
- Chatting to a friend
- Watching a DVD

Once you have a good feel as to what your idea might look like, carry out the In Your Face exercise (see pages 156–7). Once you have brought it to life, you can now engage with it by using some crafty tricks that would be way beyond the powers of Mr. Thinky Thinky.

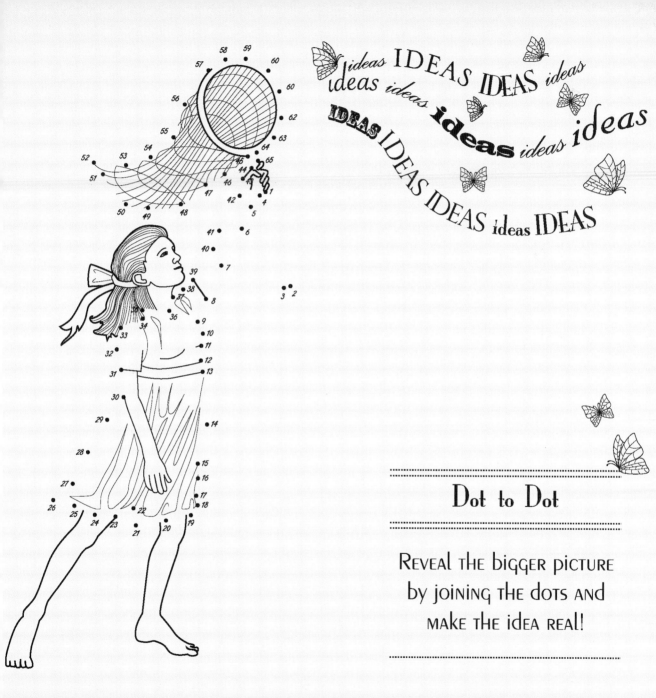

ideas IDEAS IDEAS ideas
ideas ideas ideas
IDEAS ideas ideas ideas
IDEAS IDEAS ideas IDEAS

Dot to Dot

Reveal the bigger picture
by joining the dots and
make the idea real!

GETTING REAL

Not long ago my wife Anna and I had a big dilemma. I've noticed that the bigger the decision I have to make in my life, the more intellectual to-ing and fro-ing I do. And this decision was bigger than any we had made before. It may seem like a stupid question to many of you, but to me it really needed deep introspection to make sure we were certain.

Did we want to have children or not? A lot of my friends thought this was ridiculous! Of course we did! Interestingly, these same people had children, they had made it real and had the benefit of their own deep and personal experience. We hadn't.

Now there are some people in this world who are born to have children and there are others who are not, and we weren't sure which camp we fell in to. I believed that many people have children just because it is expected of them – society norms and all that. Regardless of whether we could have children, we really wanted to know if it was truly what we wanted. Anna and I were totally smitten with each other, our careers were going great, things couldn't have been better. But we just didn't know for certain. We were anxious, confused and well and truly stuck. To escape this sticky place we needed a way to bring clarity and that was by making it REAL.

So this is what we did. We made the decision not to have children! We made it with absolute certainty so we really felt what it was like to look into the future and see our lives without them. We then went on with our lives for a week without telling anybody about our decision, just seeing what influence it made on how we lived our lives. I found myself staring at fathers with children in the park, I started looking at adverts for smaller houses. I imagined a very different circle of friends, sporty cars, more indulgent vacations, more freedom, more hedonism, but also less point, less stretch, less love.

In short, everything had changed. It gave me a different self-image, a revised sense of the future and it felt all wrong. The deciding factor was the empty feeling that we had. It's hard to describe but it was like a gnawing ache – our states were telling us that deep down we wanted children.

We then reversed the decision and noticed the difference. We felt light and energized. I felt compelled to go and kiss my wife, something that I haven't stopped doing ever since. After being out of state for seven days, getting back into state was a great indicator of how I should feel when things are on track. My god, it feels good.

By going through this simple exercise, what was once an impossible decision to make intellectually, was like black and white. It had become real. Of course, we weren't sure if we could actually have children, but at least we were now absolutely certain that we wanted to try for them.

And, I am ecstatic to say that two weeks before the writing of this chapter, our son Harvey was born.

STEPS TO GETTING REAL

1. Make the decision. It doesn't matter which one – you can swap after 7 days. Feel the decision in your bones, that it is absolutely what you are going to do.

2. Visualize what will now happen in your life; daydream and let your mind create future scenarios.

3. Live your life, but notice how you feel. Are there any times that you seem particularly triggered into a good or uncomfortable state?

4. After 7 days review your decision. What have you learnt? If it's enough to settle your decision, then do so. If not, try the same exercise on the other option (you often get the biggest reaction to the option you don't want because the one you do want feels so natural).

Or try heads or tails

    a) Simply assign the two possibilities to heads or tails on a coin.
    b) Toss it, and see what decision the universe makes for you.
    c) Notice how you feel about it.
    d) Review decision and do the one that feels great.

Still not there? Then try the Split Vote …

HEADS OR TAILS

Tim was having problems making a decision. He was a freelancer and had some down time between jobs. It was a great opportunity to get some much needed R & R. The problem was he had two options and couldn't decide which to go for.

He had weighed up the options and both looked great. One was to go and visit an old friend in the States, the other was to be crew on a yacht that was traveling from Southampton to the Mediterranean. He hadn't seen his mate for ages and missed his company. He had never been to the West Coast before and was promised a trip of abandon and hedonism. The sailing trip, however, had its own appeals: sunshine, sea, space and time!

After weeks of to-ing and fro-ing there was only one way out. He tossed a coin. Heads the States, Tails the Med. It was Heads! 'Damn!' was his response.

As soon as it became real he realized what he really wanted. He wanted to learn how to really sail and get good enough to hire his own boats every summer. The trip to America was all about letting off steam, while the boat could be relaxing and open up new avenues.

SPLIT VOTE

When a great friend of mine was totally stumped and couldn't choose between two options, she engaged with the issue from a totally different angle. She couldn't decide whether or not to go and live in Australia. So one evening she went out with a group of friends and told them all that she was going. The whole evening then unfolded around her new plans – what she was going to do, what she'd miss, etc. On another night that week she went out with a separate group of friends and told them she was staying, and again the evening unfolded to the tune of this scenario.

This process made the decision very real for her and created two very different reactions. Her state was anxious and distressed when she told them she was leaving for Australia which only increased as she started to fill in the detail. To her surprise, she felt strong and energized when discussing staying in London. It became clear to her that she didn't want to go to Australia at all – her boyfriend did.

Split Vote is an extension of 'Getting Real'.

The act of verbalizing our decisions to people who will have a view or will be impacted by it, makes us engage more fully with the decision, giving us a reaction that will help you make a choice. In truth, it's Getting Naked.

GETTING ON THE MOVE

After much monkeying around and playing with these exercises, it's likely you have something you want to do, an option to get you moving again. If right now you don't, that's cool.

As this is a creative process you never know how it will work. Sometimes we have a blinding inspiration in the first few minutes and immediately become liberated. At other times we have to dive back into the exercises. There are no rules for creativity – you make the plays.

If you throw enough energy at your concern or opportunity and are flexible enough with your approach, you will always get movement. If you have made your decision and you know what you want to do next, it's now time to engage your head and your heart.

ENGAGE YOUR HEAD AND HEART

ENGAGE YOUR HEAD – MAKE A PLAN

Some decisions are easily put in place and don't need too much thinking through. Others are more complex and long-term. These need a plan.

First, you have to be clear about what it is you actually want to do and achieve.

- How will you know when you have got where you want to be?
- What difference will it make to your life?

Then you need to chunk it down into a number of steps along a time-line. For each step ask the questions.

- 'How will I know when I have got where I want to be?'
- 'What difference will it make to my life?'

Now make it real. Bring it to life. Use pictures, symbols, whatever makes each stage and the end goal seem more exciting. And then get naked with it. Show it off. Keep it around you every day so you can see how you are doing, keeping in mind the end goal at all times.

WHENEVER YOU ACHIEVE EVEN THE SMALLEST MOVEMENT TOWARDS YOUR GOAL: CELEBRATE. FEEL THE SUCCESS IN EVERY PART OF YOU AND KNOW YOU ARE GETTING CLOSER TO WHATEVER YOUR HEART DESIRES.

WISH LIST WORKS

My wife Anna is a coach and therefore has been a firm believer in setting goals for years. It all started when she went on a workshop and as part of it was asked to write a list of wishes. Her list became an outpouring of all the things that she truly wanted – everything from where she wanted to live, to how she would earn her money, to what her partner would be like (before my time, I might add!).

Anna then brought it to life with pictures and scribbles, and then worked out how she might achieve some of these. Somewhere along our travels, her goals got filed. She recently found them. Astonishingly all of them have been achieved. Not broadly speaking but to the actual quality of the description. We now live in the house she described, she has exactly the successful career that she wished for and very spookily married me, a guy with characteristics that had been written down years before.

Needless to say, she still makes plans and sets goals, and when she reviews them every few months, there is always a surprise and therefore a celebration.

ENGAGE YOUR HEART – ENERGIZE

The success or failure of every project I have ever been involved in has never been due to complexity, demand, timing, intellect or even a fabulous plan. These don't make a project happen. It's the energy involved that guarantees success.

It's therefore essential to engage with your future success in an energized and creative state. There are many ways to get there, from plain, simple determination to Reasons to Be Cheerful (see page 187).

Remembering why I am doing it works for me.

So …

1. Take three deep breaths.

2. Visualize in your mind's eye what your life will look like when you have achieved your goal, when you have got unblocked and created momentum. What will you be doing? How will that be different? What impact will it have on your relationships? How will you now spend your time? How do you feel?

3. Drink in the whole experience. Notice the impact in all aspects of your life and how you are. Notice how your state feels.

4. Repeat the above until you can't physically restrain yourself from getting started.

MAKING IT HAPPEN

- Every morning when you get up, check in with your plan – the one that you have made Real.

- Gauge where you have got to and feel good about your accomplishment.

- Visualize your end goal and check in with that feeling of accomplishment.

- You should feel good. This is the opportunity that excites you, the one that is the very expression of who you are. Love it.

- Now, what are you going to do today that gets you a step closer to achieving it?

- Make yourself feel good about taking this step, then let rip and unleash that positivity.

- Keep doing until life never quite looks the same again.

POO STICKS!

Creativity will drive you to do things that are uncomfortable, risky and sometimes downright crazy. I came up with an idea a few years ago – one that would cost 10¢ to make, sell for over $1 and millions of people could use every day.

The idea was this. The fastest way to get rid of embarrassing bathroom odors is to light a match, and yet less than 10 percent of the population do this. This is because some don't know about it, while others feel that it's all a bit functional or even a bit odd. But what if the matches were impregnated with incense so that not only do they get rid of nasty niffs but they also leave a sweet smell behind? The idea is called 'Poo Sticks'.

For years this idea continued to bug me. No matter what I threw myself into, there was this little voice in my ear saying, 'Poo Sticks is genius! You won't know if you don't try.'

I have now trademarked 'Poo Sticks' using my own money. The next steps are to find a manufacturer, develop a business plan, talk to retailers, etc. I know there is loads to do but I am excited because I am doing something that is important to me.

I have no idea if Poo Sticks will work and a part of me doesn't mind too much if it doesn't. To me it is worth investing in a thousand ideas that might not work because I am doing what I believe in. I am keeping the dream alive.

© WillKnight_070805

YOU ARE NOW READY

Well, you've done it! You have completed the journey to this point and by now you should be feeling well pleased with yourself. You have learned a whole new set of theories, techniques and exercises, you can create sparkly opportunities simply by approaching life differently, and you know such opportunities are there for you simply by listening and attending to your state. Things have certainly moved on and you deserve to feel good.

Now you can turn your hand to Creative Life Mastery – the goal of making all that you have learnt in this book a permanent part of your life, not just a set of tools you can use when you need them. Mastery comes from doing it, from gaining experience. The more you do it, the more it becomes a part of who you are – it becomes second nature!

You need to be ready to come up with new angles and perspectives on all aspects of your life – whenever they are needed. You can't afford to wait for your next vacation to think about your life. It is happening now!

When Creative Life Mastery becomes an essential part of who you are, your life will become abundant with stimulus, opportunities will lie all around you and there will be a pervading sense of optimism.

But I promise you, with very little effort (if it takes much effort, you are doing it wrong) these skills will put you into a world of exploration, a place where you will never be bored, a life where you write your own exciting script. It might not happen overnight, but sustained creative wizardry pays off, because magic does happen and lives are never the same again.

'Everyone who has taken a shower has had **an idea**. It's the person who gets out of the shower, dries off, and **does** something about it that makes a difference.'

Nolan Bushnell, Founder of Atari

AND NOW, GRASSHOPPER ...

To get these exercises, attitudes and behaviors into your bones, do them more. Try them whenever an opportunity or challenge arises.

Do them in half an hour. Stretch them out over a luxurious week. Do them with mates. Do them with your team at work. Put a reminder in your diary to review your ideas every two weeks and reward yourself when it feels like you are creating movement. Check your state as often as you can; watch it and notice the changes. And when it feels stuck, break out.

Continually bring freshness into your life: read new magazines; go on different vacations; try different foods; take up new hobbies; meet new people; break your most loved habits. Use your world as stimulus.

Creativity doesn't start and finish. It's not just for special occasions; it's for now. It is a way of life. Creativity gives you the chance not to be wrong and not to worry about being right. You get to be playful, curious and intuitive. If things get difficult then you simply move on and find another angle. Don't be hard on yourself or take yourself too seriously. But above all, with Creative Life Mastery, life just gets more fun!

I wish you all the best with your new and sparkly future. And when you invent new ways to do this, from exercises to principles, games to state breakers, please let me know and I will save them up for the next edition.

Enjoy living your life!

Mojo Makers

INSPIRING OPPORTUNITIES

finish

IMPACT

YOU ARE HERE

INSIGHT

IDEAS

start

YOU ARE
FREE
IF YOU CHOOSE
TO BE

INDEX